Hidden Blessings from Cancer

ALAN WILLIAMS

Hidden Blessings from Cancer

ALAN WILLIAMS

Contributing Writer

Sue A. Allen

A Transformational Adventure Story

Volume 2

Copyright © 2016 Alan Williams

All rights reserved.

ISBN-10: 1533697108
ISBN-13: 978-1533697103

All rights reserved solely by the author. The author guarantees all contents are original and do not infringe upon the legal rights of any other person or work. No part of this book may be reproduced in any form without the permission of the author.

Unless otherwise noted, all Scripture references were taken from the New King James Version®. Copyright © 1982 by Thomas Nelson. Used by permission. All rights reserved.

Scripture quotations marked ESV are from the ESV® Bible, (The Holy Bible, English Standard Version®), copyright © 2001 by Crossway, a publishing ministry of Good News Publishers. Used by permission. All rights reserved.

Scripture quotations marked NIV are taken from the Holy Bible, New International Version®, NIV®. Copyright © 1973, 1978, 1984, 2011 by Biblica, Inc.™ Used by permission of Zondervan. All rights reserved worldwide. www.zondervan.com The "NIV" and "New International Version" are trademarks registered in the United States Patent and Trademark Office by Biblica, Inc.™

Scripture quotations marked MSG are taken from THE MESSAGE. Copyright © by Eugene H. Peterson 1993, 1994, 1995, 1996, 2000, 2001, 2002. Used by permission of NavPress. All rights reserved. Represented by Tyndale House Publishers, Inc.

Italics in Scriptures have been added by the author.

Cover design by Page Vandiver, Simply Heaven Design, SimplyHeavenDesign.com
Cover design by Ashley Rodriguez, hellodesigner.crevado.com.
Interior layout by Inda Williams
Photography by Inda Williams

Printed in the USA

DEDICATION

To God be the glory!

CONTENTS

	Acknowledgements	i
	Introduction	iii
1	Comfort Zone	1
2	Brokenness: The Phone Call	9
3	First Surgery Day	15
4	Hope for Healing	21
5	CaringBridge Posts	25
6	"Why?" to "How?"	29
7	Receiving the Love of God	45
8	Back to CaringBridge Posts	59
9	Resting in Spiritual Awareness	87
10	Finding Peace	95
11	Pausing to Reflect	99
	About the Author	103
	About the Contributing Writer	105
	More Stories	107

ACKNOWLEDGMENTS

First and foremost, I want to thank our Heavenly Father for strongly encouraging us to write this book and more. I am a finance major and my wife is an accounting major and communication is not one of our strong points. But God has blessed us with a wonderful contributing writer, Sue A. Allen. Without her wonderful way with words, this story would have been quite a challenge to read.

I'd also like to thank my lovely wife, Inda, for her unwavering faith and limitless patience, and for the biblical truths she has imparted to me. She is a woman with powerful prayers and limitless joy. Thanks to my awesome sons, Tyler and Dustin, and our extended family for relentless love and support throughout this journey.

Further, I'd like to thank Mike Murphy for encouraging me to open my mind to receive the limitless love of our Heavenly Father. Huge thank you to Pastor George Oakes for training me up in the grace of our Father and providing input for this book. And I'd like to acknowledge Michael and Beverly Gotcher and the LifeAustin SpiritLife leadership team for constant encouragement and prayer support. Also, I'd like to acknowledge my friend and pastor, Pastor Randy Phillips of LifeAustin Church, for bringing me in to a church body that loves and prays and for always being available for encouragement, insight, prayer, friendship and love.

Finally, I'd like to thank our Transformational Adventure Team that God brought together for such a time as this. As I mentioned, Inda and I are not gifted in communication and we have been incredibly blessed by this divinely placed team. Please see the Purpose Page on our website to see the fantastic talent God has brought together.

TransformationalAdventure.com

INTRODUCTION

Before I was diagnosed with cancer, I thought I had my life all figured out. I was successful in everything I did, which resulted in some stinking thinking on my part. I thought I knew exactly how God worked in my life as well as in the life of others. Up to this point, I relied on my physical strength. The harder I worked, the stronger I became. However, when cancer hit, my world came crashing in. The things I thought I had under control, I no longer controlled. I suddenly realized I wasn't invincible.

When I tell people that cancer was a good thing, even a blessing for me to experience, people look at me with a strange sense of bewilderment. I can almost hear them say, "Are you crazy or just plain stupid?" For this very reason, I quit telling people that my journey with cancer was one of the best things that ever happened to me. But the results are indisputable. Through the past five years, a life-changing transformation has taken place in me and within my family relationships, powerfully impacting Inda, my wife since 1982, and our two sons.

Cancer patients are in a club. Our own special club. As soon as we receive our admission ticket, we don't think anyone else can relate to our journey, which to some extent is true. However, everyone's life experiences take on various twists and turns. For me personally, God used my cancer journey as a catalyst to a life of transformation. I discovered cancer created a brokenness in me, which necessitated change. In all honesty, I may have needed to go through cancer to allow God to step in and rescue me. And graciously, He did.

This riveting story exposes the commonly placed barrier we erect between God and ourselves by dwelling on the question, "Why is this happening to me?" But there is hope. You can move forward by breaking down mindsets that limit possibilities. You can find rest in your journey by taking the best next step. Remember, God is for YOU and wants to bring peace in your heart.

In Romans 8:28 we read, "And we know that all things work together for good to those who are called according to His purpose." I clung onto this verse during this season of my life. Although I have heard many explanations of this verse, I have come to realize that I will never fully comprehend the depth of what this verse means for me. Diving in deeper and deeper is what has created our transformational adventure. And I love it! Each step of obedience helped me discover and trust God a little bit more. I would not trade any single experience in order that I may share these things with you. I pray you may learn from my story and have hope for a better tomorrow...a life of abundance in every area of your life.

In my upcoming book, **The Hidden Blessings from Chemo**, the process of physical restoration and the possibility of healing are further explored. Although the progression from losing control to total surrender under God's authority was painstaking, I have come to know that we serve a very good God. If God can restore me physically, then He can restore all areas of my life. And if God can do it for me, He can do it also for you.

Please let us keep in touch with you when new videos and Books are released by signing up on our website at TransformationalAdventure.com.

1 | COMFORT ZONE

"It may be hard for an egg to turn into a bird: it would be a jolly sight harder for it to learn to fly while remaining an egg. We are like eggs at present. And you cannot go on indefinitely being just an ordinary, decent egg. We must be hatched or go bad."[1] -C.S. Lewis

In my mind, I had reached the pinnacle of the American dream. It was the fall of 2010 and after twenty-nine years of marriage, my wife Inda and I were empty nesters easing into the next page of our life's story. Our two sons were excelling in college. Our eldest, Tyler, was close to graduating in a mere four years with a dual degree in accounting and finance. The younger, Dustin, was entering his sophomore year majoring in electrical engineering.

As a dad, I was proud of my boys. There is a degree of satisfaction in seeing your offspring succeed. And Inda and I were excitedly

---

[1] C.S. Lewis, Mere Christianity (1952; Harper Collins: 2001) 198-199.

anticipating what the next years would bring. We had plans for our future. Big plans. Plans of enjoying life and the fruit of our hard labor.

> *You do not know what will happen tomorrow. For what is your life? It is even a vapor that appears for a little time and then vanishes away. Instead you ought to say, "If the Lord wills, we shall live and do this or that."*
> *James 4:14-15*

If I were completely vulnerable, there was a degree of arrogance in my thinking. I assumed I was entitled to sit back and relax after years of strenuous labor. I believed I deserved an A+ for raising respectful, hard-working young men. I imagined a future of lounging in my easy chair and watching the sunset next to my beautiful wife.

I thought...I had arrived.

Life was really good.

And I considered putting the car into auto-drive.

I wonder if any of you can relate?

I'm a restaurant owner and pretty darn good at it. Not to brag. I'm just trying to let you see life from my personal angle. My wife and I had diligently worked hard to get our first restaurant up and running rather smoothly. We had completed several projects at the store in the past year and a half. Obtained a second restaurant. Hired and trained new team members. Added our personal touch. Everything was going according to plan.

But then, an unexpected torrential hailstorm blew through in

2009, damaging the roof, deck, and siding of our home. Rather than viewing the storm as a setback, we jumped on the opportunity to make necessary improvements and upgrades. The wooden deck was swapped for concrete and slate tile. The siding was modernized with stucco. The landscape enhanced with a personalized garden. And although the renovation was awfully painful, we saw it draw us closer together as a family.

Since it seemed like we were getting the hang of the DIY lifestyle, we purchased a cabin on Lake LBJ that needed some work. I saw it as an opportune time to escape the declining stock market and invest in some real estate instead. At least that's what I told myself and anyone else who pried. Rather than honestly appraise my selfish intentions, I justified my actions to get what I wanted. A place to get away. A spot for some rest and relaxation. Another destination to call mine.

There was a tinge of guilt.

Possibly a trace of pride.

I knew my finances could be used to expand the Kingdom of God rather than on my own extravagances.

But I didn't change my mind. I reasoned I was doing the right thing. That's what we all do when we really want something. We justify our actions rather than face the uncomfortable dissonance that is raising tension in our individual belief system. We tell ourselves we are doing the right thing and deny any negative feedback making waves in our brain. Therefore, to make myself feel better, I was convinced we would open up our cabin for use by our church. No strings attached.

ALAN WILLIAMS

How do you define the word "Christian?"

I thought I was doing enough to get by. I would've considered myself a "good" Christian. Based on my outer appearance, I was living it—walking the walk and talking the talk. I was volunteering in the men's group at our church where I spearheaded a grill team, cooking for the youth and large church gatherings of approximately 1,500 people. The men's groups were expanding and I thought I deserved partial credit. I was also on the local school board and felt like I was making a positive impact for the children and future direction of our community. Meanwhile, Inda was leading a women's Bible study group and together we served in directing a class designed to develop healthy marriages.

On the spiritual front, according to one pastor, I was considered one of the more "mature" believers in our congregation. At a minimum, I juggled two different Bible studies simultaneously: one privately and another with six men. We were studying the book of Ephesians using a Key Word Bible, which investigates definitions of significant words in the original Greek and Hebrew language. It took us an entire year to study six chapters.

I was doing everything I knew a Christian should do and despite my actions, I was inwardly dissatisfied. I didn't feel close enough to God. Although my head knowledge of Scripture was growing, I could not explain why I was struggling with discontentment. I wanted to do even more, yet unknowingly, set strict limitations on God.

Frustration was mounting.

I was hungry and unsatisfied.

Restlessness stirred in my inner being.

> *"Deep in his heart, every man longs for a battle to fight, an adventure to live, and a beauty to rescue."[2]*
> *— John Eldredge*

Men are built with warrior's hearts and I was ready to go to battle. I spent hours pondering if I would be worthy to fight in the front line of the final battle. I even told God that I was willing to be placed in the enemy fire. *What would it be like to be in the ultimate battle of good versus evil? To behold the Enemy thrown down once and for all?* My thoughts were captivated with the spiritual warfare of the End Times. My thoughts were of a future battle. But I never considered or imagined being part of the fight right now. I never made the correlation that we are joining in the fight in real time. Within the deep recesses of my soul, I longed for adventure. I wanted my life to matter, but unfortunately, I didn't know how.

Like so many, I longed for a unique purpose to fill my soul with satisfaction. At the time, I had no idea that the only thing that would ultimately fulfill and settle my soul was God Himself. Without this insight and wisdom, I kept treading on. I lived a good life. Behaved like a good Christian. Pursued my own dreams. And because it appeared that the pieces of my life were nestling nicely together, I assumed that God must be pleased with me. He must be on my side.

Since things were going my way, I thought I was doing what was

---

[2] Eldredge, John. Inside Book Cover. Wild at Heart: Discovering the Passionate Soul of a Man. Nashville, TN: T. Nelson, 2001.

right. I considered my success as a reward from God for my good behavior. It appeared I had received His stamp of approval and the blessings kept rolling in. It seemed as if every detail, every relationship, every business venture, and every spiritual milestone were being reached with ease. In all honesty, life seemed like a dream come true. I could not imagine it to be much better.

I gave God a little "g" in order to control my own destiny.

Like so many of us, I made my theology into a mathematical equation. The first part of my equation was modifying my behavior to look like a Christian should. Read my Bible. Go to church. Pray every day. Add to that, I was an exemplary citizen by leading well in my community. Based on my assumption, it looked like God was doing exactly as I pleased. For this very reason, I taught my sons to live in the same way. My spiritual barometer was measured by my financial success.

Modified Christian Behavior + Community Service =Financial Success

I thought I had all the answers and insisted my sons follow my footsteps. Paying little attention to their natural gifting, I ordered them to be just like me. Success was all that mattered. It was my agenda. Expecting nothing less, I wanted them to make me look respectable to my peers in the community and within my church. My measuring stick was labeled "Money." If I were completely vulnerable, it is what really mattered to me. I was content and settled in my comfort zone, feeling entitled to do so because of my relative intelligence. At the time, I had no idea there was a plank in my own eye. I didn't realize my self-reliance was deeply rooted in pride. I was sabotaged by my intelligence.

Unnoticeably, selfishness was slithering into all the avenues of my life. At the University of Texas, I had a very successful football coach question my teammates and me when we messed up, *"Are you going to do it my way or the wrong way?"* I adopted the style of leadership: *"MY WAY!"* At the time, I full-heartedly believed God was directing me to lead this way. If I had been successful by doing A + B, then surely others would follow my footsteps. I thought I had life all figured out.

ALAN WILLIAMS

2 | BROKENNESS: THE PHONE CALL

It was September 2010 around four o'clock in the afternoon. I came home early to get ready for the Friday night high school football game. Inda was on her way home as well. Friday night football had become our routine, even long after our boys, who played for the same Lake Travis High School team, left home. Call it our Texas tradition. We loved the enthusiasm of the home team crowd, the smell of peanuts and popcorn drifting down each aisle, and the adrenalin rush of cheering for these talented young athletes. And, quite honestly, the coaches attributed to our amusement as well. Their highly animated antics always made me smile. The teams played to perfection, winning 5 State Championships in a row, an all-time record in the state of Texas.

I loved watching the middle-school kids awkwardly talking to each other near the concession stand, and the elementary age kids running around just beyond the end zone. Plus, watching my nieces cheer. I loved the pregame tailgate party and catching up with old friends who we bonded with in our Pop Warner coaching days. Of course, I loved winning (which fortunately we did a lot), but losing wasn't the end of the world. It was always more about the entire experience.

Oh, and did I mention the chili Frito pie? One must not forget the highly caloric and mediocre mess of goo. Still to this day, I wonder why I could never resist it. Mushy chips. A bit lukewarm. Yet satisfying, salty flavor.

As I was waiting for Inda to arrive home, the phone rang. The call was from my dermatologist. Recently, I had an open wound on the bottom of my left heel biopsied. In the past nine months, I had consulted three different doctors about this nagging wound that kept growing larger. The last three visits were to a dermatologist. He gave me varying ointments to help heal the sore area, assuring me it was nothing to worry about. But the wound was increasing in size and the pain was growing increasingly greater. At my last appointment, I told him it was getting worse. I now was limping with every step and my back was hurting because my walk was altered. He told me that the wound was healing fine, but to speed up the process, he cauterized the area. While the heel was deadened, he took a biopsy and just for chagrins, sent the sample in for testing.

Looking at the caller ID, I thought to myself, *"This is a bad sign."*

I answered the phone and hesitantly exchanged greetings. His voice seemed cold and calloused. The very next thing I heard him say was, "You have melanoma." Inwardly I was screaming. *Why in the world did he wait so long to take a biopsy!* Yet I did not utter a word. The shock overwhelmed me. The gravity was heavy. He reassuringly said it is probably stage 1 that will require removal of some "material" on my heel. At this point, I wasn't sure if I could believe him.

[*Click*]. Our phone call was over.

Within minutes, Inda arrived home…but I did not share the news with her. We went about business as usual and drove to our typical Friday night game. On the way home, while sitting in the post-game traffic, I could not bear the secret any longer. The doctor's words spilled forth from me.

> *"No one loves the messenger who brings bad news."*
> *— Sophocles, Antigone*

Funny thing, Inda responded to me as I did to my doctor. She was upset and frustrated that I did not quickly respond to seeking the help of a doctor and wondered why they hadn't biopsied it earlier? Like months earlier? Honestly, who could blame her? Likewise, I was angry with myself. Nonetheless, in her own special way, I felt that she did not think this diagnosis was going to be life threatening. Like somehow her faith would be enough to carry us through. That's just the way she is.

Numbness dulled our ability to feel remorseful for what lie ahead. Rather than allow heartache to settle in, we busied ourselves with unnecessary household chores. Robotically we went through the motions of preparing for my two-month recovery period. Our busyness provided an escape from facing our unpleasant emotions. Meanwhile, the physical pain was mounting. Since my heel had a one-inch open wound, every single step was burdened. My back did not tolerate my new gait, and things kept worsening. Adding insult to injury, in my last minute preparations before surgery, I reinjured an old shoulder break. I couldn't lift my arm, couldn't sleep on my back, and couldn't walk without pain. Crap. How the heck am I going to use crutches or a walker with my shoulder like this and my back like that? This was going to be a long road to recovery.

I was referred to a specialist, Dr. Declan Fleming, who trained at the MD Anderson melanoma center. I also would see Dr. Habash, a skin graft specialist, to reconstruct my heel by rerouting nerves, arteries, and veins as he moved "material" from my instep to my heel. I find it amusing that doctors insist my body be called, "material." I guess they think it sounds less intimidating than saying the honest truth. Rather than admitting they would be gruesomely cutting body chunks off and interchanging it with other parts of my body, they simply stated they would be moving "material" about.

Preliminary testing showed that the cancer was most likely not a stage 1, but rather stage 2. Post-surgery results would give us a definitive answer. I was told this surgery may be much tougher than what I might expect and that I should be prepared. I am glad I didn't focus on how tough things might be but instead, tried to focus on trusting God to bring me through.

Spiritually, I felt like I was in a good place to receive difficult news. As I mentioned earlier, for the prior couple of years, I felt there was something missing. In the back of my mind I had wondered, *"Is this all there is to Christianity?"* I had an unexplainable peace that God would get me through this. My chance of survival was 90%+. After all, I had been here before. At the age of thirty-seven, I survived 98% blockage in my left anterior descending coronary artery and heart bypass with much lesser odds, so I was content with my chances of surviving cancer. (You may see *The Heart of It*

All story for more detail).

At that moment, I became all in, but at the time, I did not know how deep "all in" could become. To the best of my ability, I wanted to live for Him. This was pivotal. Whatever God desired. Whether I live or die, I was content to live my life for Him and to bring Him glory. I don't know if I have the words to adequately explain it. A place of contentment and peace is reached when we surrender more and more of our lives to Him. It's not a destination, but rather a trajectory of releasing more and more to God.

> *"Rejoice in the Lord always. Again I will say, rejoice! Let your gentleness be known to all men. The Lord is at hand. Be anxious for nothing, but in everything by prayer and supplication, with thanksgiving, let your requests be made known to God;* **and the peace of God, which surpasses all understanding, will guard your hearts and minds through Christ Jesus."**
> *Philippians 4:4-7 (Inda's Life Verse)*

ALAN WILLIAMS

3 | FIRST SURGERY DAY

November 8, 2010

After waking early from a restless night's sleep, Inda and I made the arduous drive to Brackenridge Hospital, one of the oldest and most prestigious hospitals in Austin. The silence in the car was penetrating. We had run out of words to say. I remember looking at a red, rusty, and repainted trash can in my waiting room. Just from the looks of it, you could tell it was timeworn. And suddenly a fearful thought found its way wiggling in, *"Would I be able to outlive this ole' rusty can or would it outlive me?"* Inda reached over and clinched my hand tight as if she could read my mind. I was incredibly thankful she was right there beside me.

Time passed slowly as pre-surgery anxiety came breezing in. The nurses came in drawing blood, taking blood pressure, and sticking me with IV needles. I was ready to just to be done.

I began changing into my overly revealing, non-manly hospital gown with a wide-open backside. Suddenly, a doctor whom I had never met waltzes into my room unbeknownst. His sidekick was an incredibly large man, probably about 6'4" tall and weighing roughly 260 pounds, who introduced himself as my nurse. I really thought he should consider playing for the NFL instead. At the moment, I wasn't even sure why they were there. To break the awkward silence, the doctor began making small talk. Trying to ease my mind, he even cracked a joke or two. But then he cut to the heart of the matter and explained that he had some good news and bad news to share.

The bad news: what he is about to do is going to hurt.

The good news: it will not last long.

Suddenly, it dawns on me why the doctor needed a nurse who looked more like a bodyguard. The doc says he doesn't like applying a local anesthetic prior to the procedure because it necessitates additional shots and extra deadening time. Before I had a chance to reconsider my options, I felt the weight of this big dude pressing most of his weight on my left shin while the doctor inserted a straw that for some unknown reason he referred to as a needle. *Did I mention that I don't like needles?* Regardless of the size. Or where they are inserted.

But let's be honest, this didn't even seem fair.

He drove the needle into the open wound that was in the middle of the pad on the bottom of my foot. Yes, it hurt. However, what really sent me sailing was the injection of a radioactive fluid into the wound. The doctor's body was shaking as he exerted pressure to push the needle into my heel. The pain was overwhelming. The bodybuilding dude, whose weight was now bearing heavily down upon me, did everything in his might to constrain me. When the doctor was finished, he explained that the radioactive substance would flow to the lymph nodes that needed to be removed. The post-surgery tests would detect if cancer had spread into the lymphatic system. When he was finished explaining the medical procedure (which at this point I didn't even care), I did my best to help him understand what an ass he was for thinking that a shot to deaden the area prior to the procedure was in the best interest of HIS time and MY expense.

A couple of hours later, I was in surgery. I've had several surgeries before and never thought of them to be that big of a deal. A little bit of sleepy medicine. A time of recovery. And before you know it, all is well. Life resumes as normal. But this surgery was different. This surgery had life long implications as to whether or not I would ever be able to walk normally again. And since I was in the restaurant business, I wondered if I could continue in my career. Cancer also left lingering questions: Is something deadly growing inside me that the doctors could miss? How do they know if all the cancer was removed? Is the lymph node clear? Even if it is clear, could there be some cancer cells hiding? Or in transit somewhere?

Visitors began showing up the day after surgery. I couldn't see the bottom of my foot, but everyone who walked in my room immediately revealed uncomfortable facial expressions. Repeatedly I was asked, *"Does it hurt?"* or *"Are you on pain medication?"* My instep was gone, a drain tube was inserted in my foot, and my heel looked like a baseball with all the stitches. Despite the strange looks, I was confident that life was finally going to get better.

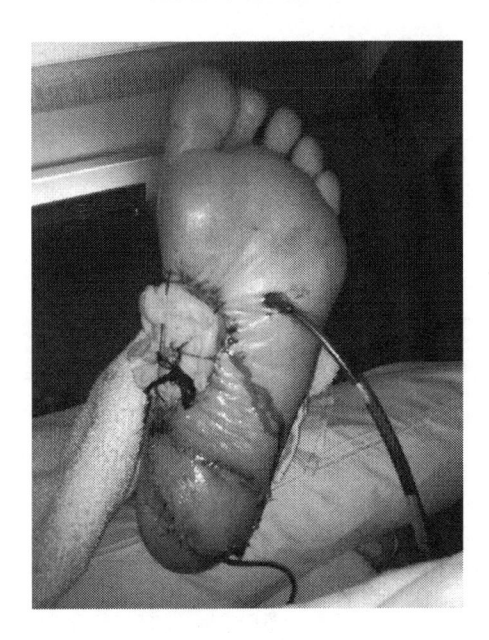

No wonder everyone who walked into my room grimaced.

A couple of days after surgery, my cancer surgeon Dr. Fleming, came into my hospital room. We exchanged greetings and this gentle, compassionate man sat down in the chair facing me. With much empathy, he said they found some melanoma cells in the lymph node that they removed, which was definitely "disturbing." In addition, they found a satellite melanoma growth in the margin of tissue they removed from my heel, which was also very "disturbing." I didn't particularly like hearing this word as it resonated deep within me.

dis·turb·ing

dəˈstərbiNG/

adjective

1. causing anxiety; worrying.

What I thought would be the end of my trip down cancer lane turned out only to be the very beginning. Dr. Fleming suggested additional procedures and referred me to an oncologist. He also suggested I get a second opinion from the renowned melanoma center at MD Anderson in Houston, just a few hours from my home. I recall being humbled by this man's sincerity. In his own right, he was incredibly accomplished in his profession and yet, he suggested another person with world class facilities may be better equipped to handle my tough situation. His utmost concern for my well-being gently reminded me that Jesus was right there by my side, guiding each step of the way.

Even when my eyesight failed to see the good abounding around me.

And my emotions were coming unglued.

My mind was racing: *Why? What? Why me? What's next?*

I needed answers. I needed peace. I terribly wanted to be restored and completely healed! What the doctors were telling me just wasn't cutting it. My head was spinning. My heart was pounding. I wanted to be left alone and yet, I wanted someone nearby. I desperately wanted help and yet, I wanted to do it all on my own. I wanted to cry but at the time, I thought that real men don't cry. I was angry. I was frustrated. And I was ~~seriously, extremely, some kind of~~...okay, I was just plain madder than mad. More than anything, I wanted to fight. I was ready to put on my boxing gloves and go to town. I just wanted to hit something...anything...to feel better! All this tension was building inside of me, waiting to explode. I needed to let go, and yet...I was holding on as best as I knew how.

ALAN WILLIAMS

4 | HOPE FOR HEALING

If you recall, I reinjured my right shoulder days prior to surgery. A few years earlier, I broke my shoulder while playing capture the flag with the church youth group. The (much younger than I) youth pastor bragged about his speed in the 40, but on this particular occasion, I was convinced I could prove him wrong. I had the angle on him and relentlessly chased him down, dove, captured his flag, landed on my elbow, expecting to body roll. Unfortunately, my expectations were miscalculated. My youth had somehow escaped me. The head of my upper arm jammed into my shoulder, crushing the bone that is over the ball joint in my shoulder. The only solace I received was the satisfaction from capturing his flag! In hindsight, it certainly wasn't worth it. For years, I encountered shoulder pain but never explored the extent of the damage until after my cancer diagnoses. And as mentioned, I felt a pop with excruciating pain jolting down my shoulder while getting some work done around the house in preparation for being immobile after surgery. Now, it seemed like my perfect world was crashing in all around me. My immediate outlook was rather depressing. Agonizing shoulder pain. Persistent lower back discomfort. Unending foot soreness. Looming cancer treatment on the horizon. It finally hit me...I can't fix this heaping mess. My life has suddenly spiraled out of my control.

In this, one of my darkest moments, I was reminded of God's provision and goodness. I received a small blessing. Praise God for whoever made a four-wheel scooter, allowing me to place the knee of my injured foot on a padded frame with handlebars, like a small trike, while relieving pressure from my injury. Oh, the comfort that scooter gave me in mobility! As a restaurant owner, being on-site is critical to the business.

My sister blessed me with a do-rag to go along with my new ride.

Days after surgery, I followed my doctor's orders and visited an oncologist, only to be the target of more disheartening news. Based on my results, he said my melanoma staging was moved up to a 3C, and I had a 26% chance of survival. He also said that I will have more lymph nodes removed in another surgery, and if they have melanoma cells, then I move to stage 4 and my chances of survival decrease significantly more.

Emotionally my mind was reeling and I found myself wanting to blame God. **I could not understand why this was happening to me.** Doubts came crashing in but thankfully Inda was standing in the gap for me. Her faith remained stable and steady. She became an incredible helper for me during all of my doctor appointments, cleaning my wounds, wrapping my foot, fixing my meals, and driving me to all sorts of places. Taking pride in my role as the spiritual leader in our home, I struggled to listen to her spiritual wisdom and advice. Despite my downcast attitude, **she continuously spoke messages of hope, encouraging me to believe that God can turn the dimmest situation around.** He alone is able.

It is He who spoke the whole world into existence and provided a way of escape for a faithful man named Noah. He opened the womb of an elderly Sarah and delivered a ram in the thicket to Abraham. It is He who parted the Red Sea and sent down manna daily from heaven. A weary, forlorn people found their way to the Promised Land by merely marching around the walls of an unfamiliar city. Shadrach, Meshach, and Abednego didn't die in the fire, nor did Daniel in the midst of the lions. Over and over and over again, Inda reminded me that God would be faithful.

> *"Now to Him **who is able to do exceedingly abundantly above** all that we ask or think, according to the power that works in us." Ephesians 3:20*

In the smallest of ways, Inda continued to sow seeds of kindness. I could not imagine how God could possibly work out my situation for good because I could not physically see it. Scripture tells us that, "Now faith is the substance of things hoped for, the evidence of things not seen" (Hebrews 11:1). Well, I guess my faith was fading. If I didn't see it, I had a hard time believing it. My faith was being deeply challenged. But God...despite my wayward thinking pursued me time and time again. He used my wife to display His unending supply of love. My laptop computer stopped working and Inda surprised me with buying one of the new Apple Mac Air computers. This seemingly small gesture spoke volumes to me! She must think I'm going to survive!

5 | CARINGBRIDGE POSTS

When you are sick, you are tired and too weary to keep up with family and friends. However, family and friends don't always get it. It's taxing to keep everyone up to date with emails and phone calls. And even then, information is misconstrued and delayed and despite best intentions, no one can perfectly put themselves in your shoes. Therefore, to avoid hurt feelings, to ward off rumors and to keep things straight, Inda and I soon started a CaringBridge website page to deliver consistent, accurate, and frequent information. Although I had no idea how my situation would turn out, I was determined in my heart to give God all the glory. I didn't want to live a wasted life...and I desired for others to know Him.

These CaringBridge posts serve as a journal of sorts. They not only give the facts accurately but also reveal how we were doing physically and spiritually at the time. I've also taken the liberty to add current reflections to some of the posts as I see things much more fully now.

November 20, 2010

We are truly blessed and thankful for the support that you all have thrown our way! Our friends and family are AMAZING! In our efforts to overcome this melanoma, we are traveling down two lanes of the same highway, with hopes to arrive at the same destination both physically and spiritually. As we travel down this road, I will update both perspectives as I feel like one does not exist without the other.

Physical Update*:*

We have been told to stay on top of all that is going on to make sure the ball continues moving forward on information transfer, doctors appointments, tests, etc. Great advice! Every doctor, nurse, and assistant have been more than willing to help in the midst of busy schedules for which, I am incredibly grateful.

At the beginning of the week, we set out to schedule as many things as possible in rapid succession in order to avoid a delay in treatment due to the quickly approaching holiday season. We had to clear an exam from my plastic surgeon, Dr. Habash, to ensure the repairs to my foot are healing as planned. It is comforting that Dr. Habash smiles every time he looks at my foot and says my healing is going very well. He released me for a treatment of cancer on Wednesday. Appointments have fortunately come together at a surprising pace, lining up together perfectly.

Spiritual Update:

On a scale of one to ten, my anxiety level is somewhere around a three. My anxiety significantly increases with the poking and prodding that must occur during the treatment processes. Some of the tests, treatments, and after-effects hurt and, not being familiar with the procedures, I don't know what to expect. Turns out that I like to be in control.

Fortunately, I have a number of people who have prayed with me and over me for healing. For my doctors. For our family (especially for Inda's continued patience with me). And for our comfort and peace. I think this is the reason my anxiety level is so low. God is amazing and He has surrounded us with many Godly people. I came to know Jesus personally in my heart (not just my head) as I was preparing to teach a youth group class. Many, including myself, thought I was a Christian prior to that moment. But I didn't really get it until that day in 2003 in my living room when a blanket of the Holy Spirit covered me in peace and understanding. I have studied and tried to absorb God's Word through much meditation and prayer, and I know I have a long way to go in my relationship with God. There are numerous things I do not completely understand, and some that I still need to surrender my life to. For the state I find myself today, to God be all the glory. I find myself rejoicing over these three Scriptures after contemplating and reflecting:

> *"So Jesus answered and said to them, "**Have faith in God**. For assuredly, I say to you, whoever says to this mountain, 'Be removed and be cast into the sea,' and does not doubt in his heart, but believes that those things he says will be done, he will have whatever he says. Therefore I say to you, whatever things you ask when you pray, **believe that you receive them**, and you will have them." Mark 11:22-24 (Emphasis mine)*

> *"The eyes of your understanding being enlightened; **that you may know** what is the hope of His calling, what are the*

riches of the glory of His inheritance in the saints, and what is *the exceeding greatness of His power toward us who believe, according to the working of His mighty power which He worked in Christ when He raised Him from the dead and seated* Him *at His right hand in the heavenly* places, *far above all principality and power and might and dominion, and every name that is named, not only in this age but also in that which is to come." Ephesians 1:18-21 (Emphasis mine)*

"Trust in the Lord with all your heart, and lean not on your own understanding; **In all your ways acknowledge Him***, And He shall direct your paths. Do not be wise in your own eyes; Fear the Lord and depart from evil.* **It will be health to your flesh, And strength to your bones.** *Honor the Lord with your possessions, And with the firstfruits of all your increase; So your barns will be filled with plenty, And your vats will overflow with new wine. My son, do not despise the chastening of the Lord, Nor detest His correction; For whom the Lord loves He corrects, Just as a father the son in whom he delights. Happy is the man who finds wisdom, And the man who gains understanding." Proverbs 3:5-13 (Emphasis mine)*

Inda and I have begun to steep ourselves in the Word of God and noticed how frequently the words faith, believe, and healing interrelate with one other. We have a prayer meeting Sunday afternoon with Mike Murphy and his wife Leslie. Thank you for your continued prayers!

Alan

6 | "WHY?" TO "HOW?"

I don't know...I don't know...I don't fully understand why things happen that are bad, difficult, and hurtful, except that we live in a fallen world. Many times I have wondered why I was the one with cancer. I questioned God, asking repeatedly what I had done wrong. In fact, a friend of mine suggested maybe God gave me cancer to teach me a lesson. When I first heard this response, it made the hair on the back of my neck stand up because I knew our Heavenly Father is good. And a good, good Father does not do harm to his own child.

> *"Or what man is there among you who, if his son asks for bread, will give him a stone? Or if he asks for a fish, will he give him a serpent? If you then, being evil, know how to give good gifts to your children, how much more will your Father who is in heaven give good things to those who ask Him!" Matthew 7:9-11*

The Bible says we have an adversary, satan, who is waiting for an opportunity to seize us. He prowls around like a lion, seeking whom he may devour. We are told he has come to steal, kill, and destroy. His primary objective is to keep us from the fullness Jesus has for us right now. And he uses his weapons with great mastery. Lies. Attacks. Lies. And more attacks. He manipulates and twists the truth, which at times, we unknowingly succumb to. As I reflect back on my life, the times I was most deceived were the times that I thought I had things all figured out…which sadly, has been the majority of my life.

A key verse I discovered during this season was when Jesus says:

> *"The thief does not come except to steal, and to kill, and to destroy. I have come that they may have life, and that they may have it more abundantly." John 10:10*

As I walked through my personal difficulties during the fall of 2010, the depth of this verse came alive for me. Plain and simple, satan works tirelessly at these three things. To steal from you. To kill you. And to destroy anything that God has established in your life. But Jesus has come so that we may have life!

This section of the book has been the most difficult to write. I have spoken with many peers and at one point or another, we all have wrestled with explaining, "Why do bad things happen?" On a macro-level, we can say we live in a broken, fallen world due to sin. But regardless, as human beings, we are prone to question one step deeper and ask God, "Why is this happening to me?"

Personally, when I was walking through the difficulties of pain and suffering, my mind was all over the place. At the time, I was facing multiple decision options and horrible treatments. I questioned my faith and the faith of others. I wondered if God would help me. I pondered whether or not this cancer diagnosis was caused by satan? Or was it the consequence of my free will? Did God give me cancer or permit me to have cancer? Am I like Job in the Old Testament when God allowed satan to attack him? Would God restore me like He did Job? Since God is sovereign, was this His will? Was cancer against His will? Where did my will start and end? Where did God's will for my life start and end? What was satan's role in all of this?

So many things. So many options. So much turmoil. I wanted to understand and have answers to all of my questions. I wanted to try and rectify my situation. If it was something I had done wrong, I wanted to make things right. But finally I came to a place of peace and contentment. As Proverbs 3:5 instructs us, "Lean not on your own understanding," I found my rest in God and God alone.

In Scripture, God uses senses to describe who He is and our relationship with Him. For example, Psalm 34:8 says, "Oh, taste and see that the Lord is good." Matthew 13:16 reads, "But blessed are your eyes for they see, and your ears for they hear" and 2 Corinthians 2:15 says, "For we are to God the fragrance of Christ among those who are being saved and among those who are perishing." Could it be God uses senses to provide deeper understanding because we can relate through first-hand experience?

Can you imagine describing the scent of fresh rain to someone who has only lived in a desert? Or what about the taste of a tangerine to someone who has never tasted one? It would be impossible for them to fully appreciate your experience if they have never experienced it first-hand for themselves. And besides, they might have a differing opinion from yours. In the same way, it is difficult to explain the deep things of God because you come to know Him and trust Him by experience. Like Job, after his time of testing and trials were completed, he said, "I have heard of You by the hearing of the ear, But now my eye sees You" (Job 42:5). In other words, I had heard of You and heard about You from the experience of others, but now I know You first-hand.

As writers and contributors, I don't know how many revisions we have written, battering back and forth, with none of us finding peace with what was written or rewritten. And I think that it may be because all of us have sought a deeper and deeper individual relationship with God and it's our uniqueness with Him as individuals that cannot be easily explained in words.

I have been praying and continually asking for God's guidance in writing this book. I finally reached a point where I desperately sought Him and asked, "Lord, what would *You* like us to say?"

And He said to me: "Tell them that I love them and I want them to come home to me!"

Wow! Where we spend eternity is far more important to Him than anything else!

Letting Him love me was the biggest barrier that I had to overcome. Opening my heart to let Him love me allowed me to love Him more. As I sought to experience a deeper relationship with God I was able to trust Him more with my all and believe in the depth of my heart that He is good.

Repeatedly in Scripture, we are told that God is always good. He is always up to something good. However, this is a difficult concept for us to grasp in the midst of such atrocities. We tend to focus on the evil or play the blame game, rather than seeing how God is working everything out for our good. Maybe the underlying struggle is with the definition of good based on our individual expectations.

How do we define the word good?

I don't have all the answers, nor can I always understand what God is up to. I cannot fully see things from His perspective. Honestly, I just don't think anyone has God completely figured out, no matter what they claim. So please don't read anything into these stories suggesting that I know what God wills, thinks, or will do in your specific situation. I don't hold all the answers. I am just telling our testimony as best I can with my personal experience in order to give you hope. My prayer is that we all grow in greater dependence on God, our Healer, Provider, and Savior.

"When times are good, be happy; but when times are bad, consider this: God has made the one as well as the other. Therefore, no one can discover anything about their future." Ecclesiastes 7:14 NIV

God loves us and He wants us to turn to Him for help. He is closer to us than I ever imagined and He wants us to seek Him. But maybe deep within, you are struggling to believe that God is real. Maybe you are wrestling to believe He cares. Maybe you doubt God can be so personal.

I want you to know that God is seeking an intimate relationship with us. Let's start right here. Take a look at the very first relationship God encountered with mankind. Adam and Eve enjoyed intimacy with God. Even after sin entered the world, God pursued knowing them so that in return, they could know Him. For God knew that the only way we could ultimately be fulfilled is in and through Him. Even when we go wayward, He is calling us near.

And they heard the sound of the Lord God walking in the garden in the cool of the day, and Adam and his wife hid themselves from the presence of the Lord God among the trees of the garden.

Then the Lord God called to Adam and said to him, "Where are you?" Genesis 3:8-9

Where are you today?

What are you looking for?

The God of the universe created you. But it doesn't stop there...He wants to be involved in your everyday. He wants to become your everything. You have been designed and wired for relationship. The kind of relationship where you are known. Your fears. Your inward struggles. Your hopes. Your dreams. This is the kind of God that I have come to know. He knows what time you set your alarm this morning, and also how many times you hit the snooze button. He knows how much you detest broccoli, and how you can never get your fill of rib eye. He knows your passion for Monday night football and your bewilderment with the purpose behind five-hour-long dance recitals. There is no one else like Him. He totally gets you!

"O Lord, You have searched me and known me. You know my sitting down and my rising up;

You understand my thought afar off.
You comprehend my path and my lying down,
And are acquainted with all my ways.
For there is not a word on my tongue,
But behold, O Lord, You know it altogether.
You have hedged me behind and before,
And laid Your hand upon me.
Such knowledge is too wonderful for me;
It is high, I cannot attain it.

Where can I go from Your Spirit?
Or where can I flee from Your presence?
If I ascend into heaven, You are there;
If I make my bed in hell, behold, You are there.
If I take the wings of the morning,
And dwell in the uttermost parts of the sea,
Even there Your hand shall lead me,
And Your right hand shall hold me.
If I say, "Surely the darkness shall fall on me,"
Even the night shall be light about me;
Indeed, the darkness shall not hide from You,
But the night shines as the day;
The darkness and the light are both alike to You.

For You formed my inward parts;
You covered me in my mother's womb.
I will praise You, for I am fearfully and wonderfully made;
Marvelous are Your works,
And that my soul knows very well."

Psalm 139:1-14

I never realized the extent of a personal relationship with God. I thought the Bible was a book to read and dissect. I read it as a book containing amusing stories. Treating it like a newspaper or a piece of great history. I never considered God's Word was alive. Nor did I realize that something written over 2,000 years ago could be so personal. The monumental shift occurred when I began expecting to hear from God. When I took a leap of faith, believing that He can. Hebrews 4:12 tell us, "For the word of God *is* living and powerful."

God is not dead or far away. We have not been left alone to fend for ourselves. I began to ponder...if God is not far away, then how close is satan?

Why didn't I understand more about the spiritual realm before this tragedy occurred? Had I been deceived?

I have heard mature Christians say that the spiritual world is more real than the physical. And honestly, I thought they were total goofballs. But now, I wonder if they were right all along. Is this how I was deceived? In the business world, a sneak attack by the rival often leaves the deceived person or company helpless and without hope. Like a hostile takeover, the deceiver is quietly buying up as much stock as possible without public knowledge. Secretly taking over the company. Leaving the deceived beaten, helpless, and hopeless.

The spiritual world must be closer than we think. Otherwise, why are these verses in the Bible?

"Put on the whole armor of God, that you may be able to stand against the wiles of the devil. For we do not wrestle

against flesh and blood, but against principalities, against powers, against the rulers of the darkness of this age, against spiritual hosts of wickedness in the heavenly places. Therefore, take up the whole armor of God, that you may be able to withstand in the evil day, and having done all, to stand." Ephesians 6:11-13

I think we can get hung up on what we think God should or should not do rather than loving Him, receiving His love, and loving other people. So many other things can distract us. Nonetheless, God is calling us into relationship. Pulling us close. Wanting us to rely solely on Him.

"I have seen everything in my days of vanity: There is a just man who perishes in his righteousness, And there is a wicked man who prolongs life in his wickedness. Do not be overly righteous, Nor be overly wise: Why should you destroy yourself? Do not be overly wicked, Nor be foolish: Why should you die before your time? It is good that you grasp this, And also not remove your hand from the other; **For he who fears** *(has reverence for)* **God** *will escape them all." Ecclesiastes 7:15-18 (Parenthesis, emphasis mine)*

The more time I spent on "Why," the more bewildered, confused, and even a bit angry I became. So, at a certain point, I decided to simply drop the "Why" and move toward the "How." I found the "Why" to be rather toxic whereas the "How" brought life to me. I no longer strive to know the "Why, Why me, or What's next?" Instead, I more frequently ask, "How? How God? How should we move forward from here? How can good be brought from my situation? How will God be glorified?" And slowly a shift is made.

"Bless the LORD, O my soul; And all that is within me, bless His holy name! Bless the LORD, O my soul, And forget not all His benefits: Who forgives all your iniquities, Who heals all your diseases, Who redeems your life from destruction, Who crowns you with lovingkindness and tender mercies, Who satisfies your mouth with good things, So that your youth is renewed like the eagle's." Psalm 103:1-5

I just need to be willing to surrender my life and receive what my Father has for me. I'm telling my Head Coach, "Put me in the game, I'm ready to play!"

And His disciples asked Him, "Rabbi, who sinned, this man or his parents, that he would be born blind?" Jesus answered, "It was neither that this man sinned, nor his parents; **but it was so that the works of God might be displayed in him**.*" John 9:2-3 NLT (Emphasis mine)*

We are not given full disclosure as to why we go through certain pains and struggles. Our ways are not God's ways and our minds are limited (Isaiah 55:8-9). We must trust that God knows what is best for us. Therefore, if you are going through any struggle in life, please move from "Why" to "How" in your thought process as quickly as possible. This is a difficult transition to make, yet critical to receiving what God has for you. He loves you more than you can fathom! He allows personalized, handcrafted, and unique experiences into our lives so that we can experience more of Him and come to greater depths of knowing who He is. For ultimately, He is after a personal, intimate relationship with you!

"...that you, being rooted and grounded in love, may be able to comprehend with all the saints what is the width and

length and depth and height—to know the love of Christ which passes knowledge; that you may be filled with all the fullness of God." Ephesians 3:17b-19

People have questioned whether God gave me this disease as a lesson. Based on my newfound relationship with God, I don't blame my Father when something bad happens to me. He is sinless and faultless, and I don't want to hinder my relationship with Him. God wants me to trust Him, which for me is harder than just loving Him. I have to trust God is working, even when I cannot see how my situation will turn around. That's what authentic faith is all about...believing when you cannot see. Trusting when you don't have answers. Following when you are blind.

"My brethren, count it all joy when you fall into various trials, knowing that the testing of your faith produces patience. But let patience have its perfect work, that you may be perfect and complete, lacking nothing." James 1:2-4

When I get to a place of proper perspective, I can trust God with my everything. I can count it all joy when trials and sufferings come my way. Not because it's going to be easy or pain-free, but rather because I know God is going to do something big. I can live with great expectancy.

November 27, 2010

Happy Thanksgiving! We have so much to be thankful for: family, friends, relationships, co-workers, our corporate offices, health, and intimacy with God! Up to this point, I have taken my health for granted. Now, I realize the blessing of health and am incredibly thankful for the healthy life I have enjoyed up to this point and the health to come.

Business Update:

Our restaurants are doing well; the team members are in place. With the leadership and ownership each person has taken, things are going just fine. We are fortunate to work with such a great group of people. There are so many in our restaurants to thank. And to be associated with such an incredible company is a tremendous blessing! I do not know how many fellow operators and corporate staff at the home office have contacted me with encouragement and prayer support. It has been very humbling and reassuring.

Physical Update:

Since the weekend, we have had three Doctor appointments as follows:

- Tuesday, Nov. 23rd: Consultation with Dr. Fleming, who was very pleased with the progress of my healing. Unfortunately, he informed us that the melanoma removed from my heel did include a "satellite" melanoma at the edge of the removed tissue. Without benefit of the PET scan results, he anticipates the standard care of treatment will be to remove all the lymph nodes in the upper thigh area, remove additional tissue from the heel, and plan Interferon chemo treatments that will last for a year. Future follow-ups and scans will also occur. Dr. Fleming is a Christian and Inda and I have been able to talk with him about how God may influence treatment.

- Wednesday, Nov. 24th: Visit with Dr. Habash, a plastic surgeon for removal of stitches and evaluation. Dr. Habash took more pictures of my foot, which is a good sign. The heel replacement is recovering wonderfully. The arch heel graft is healing as anticipated in 85% of the area. Approximately 15% did not take, but Dr. Habash is very pleased. He said I should be able to start putting pressure on the heel in another 3 to 4 weeks. Another thing to be thankful for is the knee scooter I am using to get around on!

- Wednesday, Nov. 24th: I had my PET Scan test, which translates into more poking, prodding, and uncomfortable injections. Thankfully, the people involved were incredibly helpful. I am constantly amazed at the helping hearts serving people in our health care industry. We should receive our results of the test by Monday or Tuesday, hopefully in time for our visit Tuesday morning with Dr. Ross.

Next steps:

- Tuesday, Nov. 30th: Initial consultation with Dr. Merrick Ross at MD Anderson in Houston. Dr. Ross is one of the world's most sought-after, forward-thinking leaders in the field of melanoma surgery.

- Next week, Inda and I will evaluate data and develop a game plan, including some discussions with doctors, but more importantly, seeking divine wisdom from our heavenly Father.

Spiritual Update:

Tyler and Dustin arrived for Thanksgiving and expressed their desire to spend family time together. They provide enough energy and entertainment for any situation! Our boys are amazing and we all get along so well. Inda has been unbelievably patient and helpful. I have not been able to put any weight on my foot for the past three weeks and will not be able to for at least three more. Although Inda has been chauffeuring me around since surgery, I snuck out last week. Shhh! Please don't tell. I made it to the restaurants and back and now she lets me drive by myself. I am grateful for independence like never before!

The past couple of weeks have been some of the most enlightening times of my life. Our faith and intimacy with God have grown exponentially. I think I am beginning to better comprehend how our relationship works with God. Repeatedly in Scripture, we, as believers, are called children of God. As I compare my personal relationship to God with that of my sons, the better I understand God's unconditional love. I believe that God wants His children to be obedient just as we want our children to be obedient. If we mess up, we suffer the consequences and learn lessons. As our boys have grown into young men, we have transitioned to the role of a counselor; we provide advice when asked rather than being an authoritarian in their lives. Even though we know they are making a poor decision, there is no better lesson sometimes than to sit back, say nothing, and let them learn things the hard way. In light of a parent-child relationship, I really struggled with how a good God would permit his child to be diagnosed with cancer. How in the world could God work my situation out for His good? Was I truly seeing things from His perspective?

*I "believe" God wants us to be healed. The word "believe" is used frequently throughout the Bible in our instructions as to how we should be committed to our Lord. For example, in John 3:16, "For God so loved the world that He gave His only begotten Son, **that whoever believes in** Him should not perish but have everlasting life" (emphasis mine) and in Romans 10:9, "If you confess with your mouth the Lord Jesus and **believe in your heart** that God has raised Him from the dead, you will be saved" (emphasis mine). The word "believe" in the Bible is from the original Greek word "pisteuó,"[3]*

---

[3] ""Pisteuo." *BibleHub*. Strong's Greek: 4100. πιστεύω (pisteuó) -- to Believe, Entrust. March 25, 2012. Accessed June 07, 2016.

which is defined as "entrust, with sacred significance of being persuaded by the Lord." It denotes a deep conviction, expectation, or confidence implying that what is said will take place. The dictionary defines "believe" as "think," which is so watered down in translation. Interestingly, the Greek word for "believe," "pisteuó," comes from the Greek word "pistis"[4] and is translated to our English word "faith." The two are related in the original Greek. **I am learning that the way we receive all that God has for us is to believe, submit, and surrender to the Holy Spirit.**

"Now may the God of hope fill you with all joy and peace in believing, that you may abound in hope by the power of the Holy Spirit." Romans 15:13

Jesus said, *"But the Helper, the Holy Spirit, whom the Father will send in My name, He will teach you all things, and bring to your remembrance all things that I said to you." John 14:26*

In my study, there are several instances where people were baptized in Jesus Christ and then baptized in the Holy Spirit at a different time, such as:

"Now when the apostles who were at Jerusalem heard that Samaria had received the word of God, they sent Peter and John to them, who, when they had come down, prayed for them that they might receive the Holy Spirit. For as yet He had fallen upon none of them. They had only been baptized in the name of the Lord Jesus." Acts 8:14-16

---

http://biblehub.com/greek/4100.htm.

[4] Ibid.

"[Paul] he said to them, "Did you receive the Holy Spirit when you believed? So they said to him, "We have not so much as heard whether there is a Holy Spirit." Acts 19:2

Inda and I and our family have come to believe in the Baptism of the Holy Spirit and all that the Holy Spirit has for us, but there remains so much mystery beyond our belief. More to come as the Holy Spirit teaches us.

Alan

7 | RECEIVING THE LOVE OF GOD

Reflection on prior CaringBridge Post:

At the time of preparing the CaringBridge post on November 27, 2010, I did not feel comfortable revealing the God-experience encountered by Inda and me, mainly due to my limited understanding of the individual relationship God is calling us to. Previously, I viewed God sitting in heaven on a throne up high, much like Abraham Lincoln at the Lincoln memorial. Stoic. Majestic. Royal. Untouchable. I imagined we would enter the throne room somewhat scared, seemingly small, and insignificant, almost like a bunch of ant-like creatures making our way in one at a time. Then, God would give us a nod of acceptance, acknowledging that we made it into the pearly gates of eternity. Or, with the toss of His head, He would reject us, sending us to hell. I still don't really know what heaven will be like, but the relationship I have discovered is much greater and richer than anything I previously realized.

Mike Murphy is a man we have known for over ten years. He was an assistant coach for our older son in a select basketball league and when we played on Sundays, he preached a message for the kids. As our boys entered middle school, Inda began facilitating the Fellowship of Christian Athletes program. For our first meeting, she invited Mike to speak to the middle and high school students in a large youth room in our church while we, the parents, had an organizational meeting in another room. During our meeting, a parent who was helping in the youth room darted in and boldly interrupted. With eyes wide-open, clearly in a frenzy, she whispered loudly, "You all have got to see this!" As we entered the youth room, a charismatic black man (a.k.a., Mike Murphy) stood in a sea of white kids praising and glorifying God, placing his hands on student's heads, and speaking words of knowledge[5] and prophesying words of revelation[6] over these kids. I was dumbfounded. There was no way he could know this level of detail about each person he spoke to on an individual basis. No way! I had never experienced anything like this before. Nor had anyone else in the room to my knowledge.

---

[5] "Word of Knowledge" means the ability of one person to know what God is currently doing or intends to do in the life of another person. It can also be defined as knowing the secrets of another person's heart. Wikipedia.com.2016. https://en.wikipedia.org/wiki/Word_of_Knowledge (25 April 2016).

[6] "Word of Revelation" means an act of revealing or communicating divine truth; something that is revealed by God to humans. Mirriam-Webster.com. 2016. http://www.merriam-webster.com/dictionary/revelation (25 April 2016).

Mike was loud. He was yelling...and yelling was unfamiliar within the walls of our church that we attended at that time. I contemplated whether or not to tackle him off the stage or join in. But I found myself mesmerized and unable to do a thing. Instead, I listened and watched as a number of tearful, raw, eager, and joyful students opened their hearts to Jesus. By the end of the evening, there was not a dry eye in the room. It was absolutely amazing! All of us were seeking a greater understanding of our relationship with God.

According to 1 Corinthians 14:22, prophecy serves as a sign for believers. Never before had I experienced a clear demonstration of God working in my midst. I saw with my own two eyes the conversion of numerous unbelievers, which is why Paul says this gift of prophecy should be used when "unbelievers or outsiders enter" (1 Corinthians 14:23). Wow. As the Holy Spirit worked in this room...

> *"the secrets of his heart are disclosed; and so, falling on his face, he will worship God and declare that God is really among you." 1 Corinthians 14:25 ESV*

In my current situation, I was desperately seeking greater possibilities of what God might do. I wanted to survive cancer and be completely restored. I was afraid of enduring the side effects of chemo treatment over the upcoming year. I reached a point where I realized I no longer was indestructible. Cancer was much bigger than me.

I called Mike Murphy to pick his brain about my recent cancer diagnosis. After all, he seemed to have a direct link with God. He invited Inda and me over for dinner so that we could talk more.

Mike and his wife, Leslie, explained that God wants to have a personal, intimate relationship with each of His children. Digging deeper, we began to walk through Scriptures written by the Apostle Paul, including the book of Acts and Romans. The Apostle Paul and the disciples had such amazing faith and divine power, which quite honestly, perplexed me.

They walked us through examples of healing in Scripture, performed by both Jesus and the disciples over 2,000 years ago. I was confused and puzzled. Over the years, I had studied famous authors and Bible teachers who said miraculous healings by God have ceased in our day. "God doesn't need to prove Himself anymore." I had been taught that miraculous healings were limited to Jesus, the disciples, the Apostle Paul, and a tight group of close authoritative leaders from the first generation church. Then, I was told, all miracles ceased.

When Mike and Leslie told me an opposing view suggesting that God does heal today, I became very hopeful. They explained that God still works miracles today by the Holy Spirit. He does so through ordinary believers and such work is not limited to Jesus and certain apostles. According to Galatians 3:5, "Therefore He who supplies the Spirit to you and works miracles among you, does He do it by the works of the law, or by the hearing of faith?"

Mike walked me through numerous Scriptures, beginning in the Old Testament where the Prophet Isaiah foretold of the coming of Jesus (approximately 700 B.C.). Isaiah told us Jesus was coming to so that "...by His stripes we are healed" (Isaiah 53:5). This verse is referred to again in the New Testament in 1 Peter 2:24, after the death and resurrection of Jesus.

"By His stripes we are healed." What does this possibly mean?

I had been taught about the Trinity: God, Jesus, and the Holy Spirit. I knew God the Father and Jesus as my Lord and Savior, but I really didn't know the Holy Spirit like I know Him today. I really never thought about the Holy Spirit as a separate person of the Trinity, with specific roles and purpose. Mike helped me understand that Jesus left so He could send the Holy Spirit.

> *"And I will pray the Father, and He will give you another Helper, that He may abide with you forever." John 14:16*

The Helper's name is the Holy Spirit and He takes up residence in us as believers. It is He who helped open my eyes to see God still heals today. As a result, my heart was open to receive what God had in store for me His love and His healing!

> *On one occasion, while He (Jesus) was eating with them, He gave them this command: "Do not leave Jerusalem, but wait for the gift my Father promised, which you have heard me speak about. For John baptized with water, but in a few days you will be baptized with the Holy Spirit." Then they gathered around him and asked him, "Lord, are you at this time going to restore the kingdom to Israel?" He said to them: "It is not for you to know the times or dates the Father has set by his own authority. But you will receive power when the Holy Spirit comes on you; and you will be my witnesses in Jerusalem, and in all Judea and Samaria, and to the ends of the earth." Acts 1:4-8 NIV (Parenthesis mine)*

> *"When the day of Pentecost came, they were all together in*

one place. Suddenly a sound like the blowing of a violent wind came from heaven and filled the whole house where they were sitting. They saw what seemed to be tongues of fire that separated and came to rest on each of them. All of them were filled with the Holy Spirit and began to speak in other tongues as the Spirit enabled them." Acts 2:1-4 NIV

In my desperation of wanting to be healed, my mind cracked open ever so slightly. Maybe I didn't have God all figured out. Maybe I had placed restrictions on Him. Maybe I didn't understand all that God does or doesn't do in our lives today, or how close He really wants us to be to Him. Maybe I wasn't a so-called "mature believer" for I realize now that I am still learning.

Did my mind limit the depth of relationship with God, my Heavenly Father? Could it be that I also limited my ability to receive what God so freely had to offer?

I began to challenge what I had previously been taught. What if God still healed today? Could it even be possible? And if so, maybe God would heal me!

We began to study Romans 8:6, "For to be carnally minded is death, but to be spiritually minded is life and peace." Another version says it this way, "So letting your sinful nature control your mind leads to death. But letting the Spirit control your mind leads to life and peace" (NLT). Could it be that I was not being receptive to spiritual things? Had I built up a wall, restricting what God could do? While I have never been accused of being the sharpest tool in the shed, I have used my mind for personal gain rather than the things of God. A light bulb went off. Maybe I was relying on my intellect, rather than taking a leap of faith. Maybe I wasn't praying for healing because I had placed limits on God.

Our carnal mind is our sinful nature getting in the way. Maybe today you find yourself afraid to ask God for healing. Maybe, like me, you think God no longer heals. Maybe your unbelief is inhibiting the Holy Spirit. I wonder what would happen if we simply pray. Pray for God to help us with our unbelief (see Mark 9:23-25). Pray for God to give us boldness (Hebrews 4:16). What if we would simply take a leap of faith and ask God to do the impossible?

> *"... you do not have because you do not ask." James 4:2b*

Many of us avoid seeking God because we don't want to be disappointed. Or possibly, we don't want to look weak if healing doesn't occur. Or perchance, we don't want to make God look bad. We find our faith is small.

Authentic faith occurs when what we believe with our intellect becomes real inside of us.

But worse yet, maybe we don't even care. Apathy may be the biggest battle of all. Apathy says that I am uninterested, indifferent, and unconcerned. When a person reaches the epitome of apathy, they lose sight of hope. They just want to die. They become self-absorbed, misplacing their concern for the spiritually lost and dying in this world. Unfortunately, they forget that they themselves are God's workmanship. They are handcrafted and designed by the very hands of God.

As long as we have breath in our lungs, God has something for us to do. He has created us to be participators in His great work. He has created us with purpose in mind. Now I find that pretty darn cool! God certainly doesn't need our help, for He is self-sufficient without us. But He wants us to be the hands and feet of Jesus to help each other, to love each other, and to work in unity. Regardless of your age, your income, your heritage, or race...God has planned for you to be His helper.

> *"For we are His workmanship, created in Christ Jesus for good works, which God prepared beforehand that we should walk in them." Ephesians 2:10*

However, despite what I read in God's Word, I wrestled with doubt.

I struggled to believe God could heal me.

Or that He would even want to.

Personally, my biggest battle was with my self-worth. Could the God of the grand universe care this much about little ole' me? In my football playing days, you had to perform to get playing time out on the field. In the business world, it wasn't much different. It was all about the bottom line. If you wanted to receive a pat on the back from the CEO, you had better put in long hours and have a proven track record. In order to stand out above all the rest, you must earn your recognition. Climb the corporate ladder. Be worthy of a promotion.

I considered God the boss of all bosses. In doing so, I thought I had to earn my healing. And since I wasn't sure what God thought of me at the time, I wasn't so sure He would heal me. Possibly my biggest struggle was with believing in my heart of hearts that God truly loved me and wanted me to be made whole.

That particular night, Mike directed my attention to the story of

King Asa found in 2 Chronicles. This King of Judah made a pact with the enemy army, Syria, rather than seeking help from the Lord. God became displeased when Asa tried to find his own remedy by taking matters into his own hands. A prophet attempts to convince Asa of his folly, showing that he, of all men, had no reason to doubt God's magnificent power. During his reign, God had granted peace to his kingdom.

Seeking God first should always be our first recourse. Why, it is foolish to turn anywhere else but to Him. However, more often than not, we too seek to trust in the things we can see, rather than trusting in the Lord!

Two years before his death, Asa became diseased in his feet. Failing to turn to God for help, he solely sought the aid of physicians. In the following reproof, we see the sinful heart of King Asa ultimately exposed. We see a man who trusted in humanity more than He trusted in God Himself. He looked to mankind for answers before seeking God. His misplaced expectations were on mere man, not realizing that ultimately all healing comes from the Lord.

> *"For the eyes of the LORD run to and fro throughout the whole earth, to show those Himself strong on behalf of those whose heart is loyal to Him. In this you (King Asa) have done foolishly; therefore from now on you shall have wars."*
> *2 Chronicles 16:9 (parenthesis added for clarity)*

This verse resonated deeply. I wanted to be fully committed to God. So that night I asked God to strengthen my heart. I humbly prayed, "Lord, if You determine to heal me, I will commit the rest of my days to you!" And I thought to myself, "Help me, Lord, know what it means to live fully committed to you."

During our visit with the Murphys, Leslie prayed for Inda and me at their kitchen table and then we moved to the family room where there was a piano. Mike began playing and singing worship songs. It's hard to describe the depth of the relational worship music he was singing at the time, but I have learned to understand that style of music is often called a "soaking." It was like soaking in the presence of God. I felt God's presence in the room greater than any time in my life up to this point. As we were worshiping, Mike encouraged me to open my mind and ask for the Holy Spirit, so I did. Mike was facing away from me and could not see me as he played. As I prayed to the Holy Spirit, Mike said, "There He is, there He is, open your heart and mind." Then he started laughing and "BOOM!" I felt this explosion of ecstasy and euphoria fill the upper right side portion of my chest.

I began laughing and crying at the same time. Mike told me to start moving my tongue and speaking and I cannot fully describe what came over me. I began speaking in tongues! And as I spoke in tongues, I felt the Holy Spirit fill my chest even more. This experience was greater than anything that I have ever experienced in my life, including the time that I felt Jesus enter my heart seven years earlier. It was much better than anything I had tried to fill myself with before. God blessed me, graced me, and gave me a new fullness of the Holy Spirit.

Then everyone in the room laid their hands on me and began praying for me to be healed of cancer. Inda placed her hand on my shoulder while she prayed. I could feel my shoulder crunching and popping, and Inda could feel it too. Immediately, my agonizing, persistent shoulder pain was gone and I had about 90% mobility.

Prior to the prayer, I could not raise my right arm but a few inches off of my side. After the prayer, I was able to pick up my mobility scooter with my arm fully extended in front of me. I could not explain it...my shoulder was miraculously healed! Something even bigger happened at this moment. I began to believe that healing was real, and the hope of God healing me of cancer became a genuine possibility.

Mike Murphy and Alan Williams

God could possibly heal me of cancer.

Since then, I have spoken with others who have had a similar encounter and it seems that there are varying degrees of how powerful the experience is; but He is the same Holy Spirit. Inda describes her experience as simply a greater level of surrender. My initiation to the gift of tongues was overwhelmingly powerful, maybe because I was seeking God with "all of my heart, all of my soul, all of my strength, and all of my mind" (Luke 10:27). I desperately wanted God more than anything else at this time. I wanted to be healed and to live life to the fullest, experiencing more and more of Him.

I wonder if we seek the things of this world, like alcohol, drugs, power, possessions, and sex outside of marriage, rather than God because we have never experienced Him in such a deep, intimate way. Does the enemy deceive us to seek the things of this temporal world rather than be filled with the Holy Spirit? The Holy Spirit empowers us for ministry (Acts 7:55), renews our worship and thanksgiving (Ephesians 5:19-20), restores our relationships with others (Ephesians 5:21-6:9), and convicts us of sin (John 16:8). Never before had I experienced such a deep spiritual renewal spurred on by sincerely repenting, earnestly seeking, and wholeheartedly committing my life to do His will. I believe satan will do anything to prevent us from entering into this deep intimacy with God. Deceit, distraction, and temptation are just a few of his subtle tactics.

Funny thing, Inda had already come into this deeper relationship with the Holy Spirit a year earlier. I didn't understand it and as the spiritual leader of the house, told her to stop listening to those weird televangelists who believed in that mystical stuff, including healing. I thought she was dividing us by listening to such craziness. The baptism in the Holy Spirit, speaking in tongues, and other manifestations of the Holy Spirit were things that I could not comprehend and therefore, I thought they were not of God. I thought I sufficiently knew how God worked and anything contrary to my belief system had to be wrong. Wow, my mind was in the way of the spiritual.

I had put a box around God.

I never realized how I gave Him restraining orders.

I never saw how in my own way, I was telling God what He could and could not do.

I had never considered that the miracles of old, like the parting of the Red Sea, must've come as a surprise to the beholders. How many people would stay standing on the riverbank? Never escaping the Enemy? Never trusting God to lead their way.

"Do not quench the Spirit." 1 Thessalonians 5:19

Looking back, I quenched the Holy Spirit by inhibiting Inda's spiritual growth and relationship with God. It was the most hurtful thing that I could have ever done. Thankfully, she forgave me. After I was diagnosed with cancer, the Holy Spirit used her to be my helper, my teacher, and my comforter. God worked through her in mighty ways, all the support I could ever hope for. Please see her book, **The Power of a Caregiver**, for more information.

ALAN WILLIAMS

8 | BACK TO CARINGBRIDGE POSTS

November 30, 2010

MD Anderson Cancer Center is incredible! From the first person we met at the information desk to the security guard riding in the elevators, receptionist, nurses, PAs, and doctors. Why, I even appreciate Mary who stuck me with a needle after needle, drawing nine vials of blood! It is plainly evident that these people truly care for their patients! I even heard our company's response, "My pleasure" from one of them!

Physical Update:

Today we met Dr. Ross, most likely the best melanoma surgeon in the world! Man, he was impressive! Dr. Ross seemed pleased that my cancer levels were where they are (and not any higher) but, with the melanoma satellite and the one removed lymph node that had cancer cells, he also confirmed the severity of the cancer as Stage 3C. The good news is that this may qualify me for treatment, after any surgeries, in a clinical test that may have some positive outcomes. He also has requested to have an MRI of my brain done soon to make sure "nothing is up there" (not my words). Based on my relatively "young" age...thank you, Dr. Ross, I knew I liked you from the get-go...and decent health and attitude, he suggested being very aggressive with treatment as follows:

- ➢ Remove a small section off of my heel that was near the satellite melanoma.

- ➢ In the same surgery, remove lymph nodes in my upper thigh area that will result in fluid build up in my leg. I will need to wear compression stockings daily, use a machine to massage the fluid movement in my leg, and most likely not be able to stand on my feet for more than 3-4 hours per day for the rest of my life.

- ➢ After the lymph nodes are removed, my thigh muscle will be sliced and reattached to my pelvis to cover the exposed artery in my leg.

- ➢ Perform a limb perfusion on my leg. The doctor's concern is that the melanoma on my heel and the cancer cells in the lymph nodes of my upper leg area have resulted in undetected cancer cells in other parts of my leg. The Limb Perfusion would essentially section off the blood supply to my leg and run a chemotherapy treatment to this designated area, my left leg, which would help reduce the risk of reoccurrence. This would be a one-time surgery. Hallelujah!

- ➢ Identify a post-operative treatment.

Spiritual Update:

Inda and I firmly believe that God healed me of cancer this past week. In fact, I would go so far as to say I know I have been healed by faith and the working of the Holy Spirit! Fortunately, God provided the world's leading melanoma surgeon to advise me of the best procedures. How do faith and medicine intersect? Do we rely totally on the healing that has occurred and ignore modern medicine, or contrarily, do we trust that God has directed our steps to the best of the best? Or do both positions work together simultaneously? All we want to do is honor and glorify God! How do we do it? By following God's lead every step of the way. Day by day. Week by week.

> *"The LORD makes firm the steps of the one who delights in him." Psalm37:23 NIV*

I have never been one to quit or stop short of the best possible outcome of something I am passionate about, and this tops anything I have ever experienced in my lifetime. I welcomed Dr. Ross's prognosis and treatment. In my mind, I want to move forward with the surgery. Is this where God wants my heart to go? Three weeks ago, after we found out the extent of cancer and before this faith journey started taking root, I had hoped to find the most aggressive treatment and to tell the doctors "Give me everything you have to combat this thing and then give me more." But interestingly, cancer has changed me. Rather than doing things my way, I am seeking for answers from God's Word.

Inda and I will be searching for wisdom and discernment from the Holy Spirit. Matthew 17:21 says, "However, this kind [of faith] does not go out except by prayer and fasting." For anyone who knows me, I don't like to miss a meal (at least not intentionally), but I am thinking I might need to skip a few to gain some clarity and increase my faith. This thought occurred to me after my doctor's visit today. Coincidentally, hitting me just after Inda and I had made plans to have lunch at our favorite seafood place we enjoy with family in Lake Jackson. Her instant remark, "Can't you pick anther day to start this fast?" Nope, I didn't. I am so hard headed!

If anyone is praying, please ask for wisdom, clarity, discernment, and especially faithfulness.

Thank God for you!

Alan

December 3, 2010

Inda and I are overwhelmed and humbled by the individual communication and broad support received through this website! Thank you so much for the inspiration you are giving my family and me! You all are an incredible blessing!

Physical update:

I am glad some of you find humor with the MRI of my brain, which was performed on Thursday. Inda said she was sure they would find a brick. Yesterday, I received a call from Mary at Dr. Fain's office with my MRI results and she says, "Mr. Williams, your MRI came back clear." I asked if they found anything in there and she paused, then started giggling and said, "We did find a bunch of little chickens and they were saying 'Eat More Beef.'" She then started giggling uncontrollably and I could hear the office staff laughing behind her. After several minutes, we were finally able to regain our composure and she replied, "I can't believe I said that, please forgive me." Thank God for His joy in the most unusual places! Anyway, all that to say, more great news and answered prayer for a clear MRI result. Once again, thank you.

We will go to MD Anderson on Thursday, December 16th to meet with Dr. Ross and his team for an exam and to develop a game plan for surgery that is scheduled for December 20th. Dr. Ross will have postoperative treatment recommendations once he investigates my type of melanoma and investigates all options, one of them being a possible clinical test if I qualify. A year of Interferon is the most common recommendation, but the risk reduction does not seem optimal considering the potential side effects.

Spiritual Update:

What a spiritual ride this has been the last few days! As my relationship deepens with God, I know I need to surrender to His will. I know that is His utmost desire. And I want to submit to do whatever it is He asks of me. A few years ago I came up with a purpose statement for my life that says, "To unselfishly do what God wants me to do, in a way that Jesus tells me to treat others with passion, energy, and persistence."

Although I stray frequently from this statement, it is my compass. This past week I have been struggling with my measure of faith. In my mind, I am over-analyzing what God wants me to do. Specifically, I am struggling to determine:

- Do I rely on the healing God has already given, or
- Do I rely on the surgeon that God has so gifted, or
- Do I rely upon both?

Since I learned about this cancer thing, I have been growing in my relationship with the Trinity: God the Father, Jesus, and the Holy Spirit. About mid-week, I discovered I was missing out on things God had for me. I had become double minded in my spirit. James 1:6-8 says, "But let him ask in faith, **with no doubting**, for he who doubts is like a wave of the sea driven and tossed by the wind. For let not that man suppose that he will receive anything from the Lord; he is a double-minded man, unstable in all his ways." For a couple of days, I was letting the evil one get a foothold. I was chasing so many things in my mind and as a result, I lost some of *my joy and peace, which virtually eliminated my ability to receive or give God's love.*

Jesus wants us to have peace! He said to a woman in Luke 7:50, "Your faith has saved you. Go in peace." The "God of Peace" is mentioned in 1 Thessalonians 5:23, as well as, in other places in the Bible. 1 John 4:16 says, "God is love, and he who abides in love abides in God, and God in Him." WOW! 1 Corinthians 13:13 says, "And now abide faith, hope, love, these three; but the greatest of these is love."

Inda and I have peace because we believe that God gave us the Holy Spirit for healing and we should not limit His ways of healing. Oh, my immature faith! As God's children, we should recognize and honor the gifts He has given each of us so that we may also honor God. Romans 12 has revealed to me how different we all are in how God made us and therefore, we should respect each other's spiritual gifts from our heavenly Father. We have been given these gifts so we may be unified in the kingdom's purpose. Unity was the theme of Jesus prayer in the Garden of Gethsemane in John chapter 17. We are here to help each other because we need help! Therefore, we will be welcoming the healing gifts of Dr. Ross, as well as the healing gifts of the Holy Spirit, because God has given it all to us.

What a comforting thought, especially as I find my faith wavering. We are either getting stronger or weaker in our faith, never staying the same. In this culture full of creature comforts, it is so easy for me to become complacent and gradually slip away. Then the most unexpected gift comes at me, like melanoma, to grow my faith! Fortunately, I know that one day I will be healed in entirety when my feet reach my heavenly home. For now, I just need to look for the lesson God wants me to learn in the process. In every experience, there is always a lesson.

Everyone has a different measure of faith. No one can determine what that is for another or how it looks individually because it is a personal, individual relationship that God wants with each of us. He is looking for intimacy. The greater our faith and trust in Him, the greater we will experience the fruit of the Spirit as described in Galatians 5:22-23, "But the fruit of the Spirit is love, joy, peace, longsuffering, kindness, goodness, faithfulness, gentleness, self-control. Against such there is no law."

If you have time, please pray for the following:

- ➢ Thank God for the healing that has taken place.
- ➢ Request for a cleansing and removal of all cancer cells.
- ➢ Pray for no complications.
- ➢ Pray for the surgeon's hands, open heart, and wisdom.
- ➢ Pray for my family to grow in God's likeness.

Thanks so much and God bless you!

Alan

Reflection:

I felt very much like a wandering Israelite. I just wanted to get out of there. I thought if I could find my compass, I could navigate my route to the Promised Land. After all, the manna was tasteless, nothing like I imagined God would provide. I was tired of living this story. I wanted a different ride.

Restless.

Frustrated.

Wanting to hurry God along.

I reviewed the doctor's orders over and over again in my head. I anxiously searched for an answer. What if's posed a constant threat in my head. I begged God to take this cancer from me. I told Him I would live differently. It felt like He wasn't hearing my prayers. At times, I wondered if He was still there, or was He completely done with me.

There were numerous times when I tried to take control. I thought if I prayed more, read my Bible more, told others about God more, then I could muster up enough faith to be healed. Maybe I needed to do some good deeds. Or maybe I needed to ask someone more spiritual, like my pastor, to come and pray for me. Maybe they could reach God on my behalf. I searched and searched for an answer, rather than patiently resting in the wilderness, waiting for God's response to come.

In His silence, He was still working. I just didn't realize it then. He was molding and shaping and scraping off parts of me, in order to teach me to trust. It's much easier to hear God when the answer is loud and clear. But when His presence is barely recognizable, will we turn to the whisper in the room?

I have learned when we come to the end of our rope, we discover that Jesus is our Only.

"But now, O LORD, you are our Father; we are the clay, and you are our potter; we are all the work of your hand."
Isaiah 64:8 ESV

December 11, 2010—A Post from Inda

Hello! Not a lot has happened since our last post but yet a lot HAS happened! Alan & I both lost our peace at one time or another last week (yes, satan is very real). But with the help of the Holy Spirit, your postings, and awesome friends and mentors, we were able to reclaim our blessing of peace! God is so good! His peace absolutely DOES surpass understanding!

We've been loved on, hugged, uplifted, graced, and blessed with a whole ton of prayers! I have to say that your prayers of support have brought us so much comfort and joy. It's really hard to be down when you know that you are loved so much! We can't thank you enough for your love & support!

Physical Update:

Alan overdid it and caused his foot to swell, resulting in some separation between his graft and the rest of his foot! Rightly so, he's been put in time-out!

Spiritual Update:

Alan reclaimed his peace! Alan is a doer. He's tenacious. Whatever he does, he gives it all he's got and does it well. However, he was struggling with accepting his healing in Christ. You see, it is not Alan's nature to just sit back and let things happen! He wants it done right now. After meeting with a minister regarding his frustration, he was able to come to a place of peace. This minister reminded him that we live in a fallen world and God doesn't operate on our timetable. Alan doesn't run his restaurants on faith alone (although that is a HUGE part of it). He goes to work nearly every day, except for Sunday. He is actively involved in the process.

So sitting back and waiting for God to do something isn't necessarily easy. We are taking one step at a time. And in the meantime, we will thank God for the healing He has already caused and for the healing to come. Alan will remind himself of the divine appointment with the best melanoma surgeon in the world! We cannot ignore the blessings that have already occurred!

With all that being said, Alan, the boys, and I have grown exponentially in our faith. Just when you think you're filled to the rim, your cup gets even bigger! It's been a transformational adventure! We are worry-free and confident in the eventual ending of this trial, and look forward to many long, happy years with several grandchildren to love on!

So thank you, once again, for filling us full of joy and comfort with your postings and prayers! We love you all!

Inda

December 16, 2010

Well, it's time to kick some melanoma butt! We had such a great day at MD Anderson yesterday. Dr. Ross and the staff are first-class and I don't think they take any prisoners when it comes to a battle against cancer. We spent a full day meeting different specialists who will be involved in my surgery.

As a former lineman in football, I was used to following the quarterback's lead. A play would be called, telling me what defensive guy I needed to block. I didn't need to know the entire game plan. However, Inda is not built this way and she does need to know the game plan, resulting in a lot of minutiae. I probably learned more than I really wanted to know about what is going to *happen in surgery and the side effects. But I am very fortunate that God gave me such an awesome wife and together we balance each other out. She is incredible and I am blessed to have her by my side.*

Physical Update:

On Wednesday, I met with Dr. Habash, my plastic surgeon. He was VERY pleased with the healing of my foot and said I should start applying weight on it. If you recall, around 15% of the grafts appeared as if they didn't work. Well, guess what? They did! Thank you, God! The inflammation from last week caused a minor disturbance in the tissue, but now is healing well.

Dr. Ross and company will perform an isolated limb perfusion with chemotherapy treatment, remove additional margin and material on my heel, and eliminate lymph nodes in my upper thigh area. This procedure is a fairly lengthy process. Thus, my first procedure is scheduled to begin at 9:30 am, continuing throughout the day. Dr. Ross said he will likely finish sometime around 6:00 pm.

I will likely be staying 4-5 days in the hospital after surgery mainly to monitor my blood counts and muscle recovery as a result of the chemotherapy treatment. Since the level of chemo concentration is 10 times the normal level for this procedure, lots of cells, both good and bad, will be killed. They want to ensure that the muscles do not die, which could cause amputation. So I will stay as long as they want me too! I will go home with drains and will likely recover for 8-12 weeks from the treatment. Post-surgery treatment discussions will occur 4-6 weeks from now, likely including either interferon that typically makes people feel sick for a year, or a new experimental vaccine that has no reliable track record.

Spiritual Update

God is so awesome! I truly believe I have been healed from cancer and this is a cleansing that will prevent any future cancer development. The amazing thing that God has done in this process is to bring people together by rekindling relationships in efforts of encouragement. Inda and I have been amazed and humbled at the support, uplifting messages, and acts of kindness. From dinners to notes, guestbook messages to emails, and to God moments when people I see ask what I am doing on my scooter. To pastors of local churches who have reached out and consulted with prayer groups...we are beyond words of gratitude and thankfulness! A real treat occurred on Tuesday when some former and current members of the praise band from Lakeway Church and friends came over and had dinner together and worshiped our Lord for a couple of hours! An amazing, uplifting experience at a perfect time!

Praise & worship in my home – a very special moment!

During my hospital visits, I have noticed that the front line people are the real heroes, creating such a welcoming experience at the reception desks and likewise, the nurse aids and many others making me feel right at home. I never realized the tremendous ministry of people working in the healthcare industry, impacting lives one-on-one. So many of them obviously have a strong measure of faith that exudes from their pores. They welcome in the presence of the Holy Spirit, making MD Anderson feel unique and special. I don't know where their leadership stands in regards to faith, nor do I know their personal interest in helping others. But as a businessman, I know that performance is usually a reflection of the leadership.

In John 17, Jesus prays His last recorded major prayer while in the Garden of Gethsemane, hours before his capture to be taken to His trial and persecution. Last year, these passages really hit me hard. In verse 1, Jesus prays, "Father, the hour has come. Glorify your Son, that your Son also may glorify you." His utmost desire is to bring glory to God, knowing full well it means dying. His prayer continues by making a petition for his disciples, that they may have the joy of Jesus fulfilled in them, be sanctified in the truth, be protected from the evil one, be rooted firmly in God's Word, and be one with each other so that the world can be assured that God sent Him. Jesus continues to pray to His Father for future followers and generations to come in verses 20-23, "I do not pray for these alone, but also for those who will believe in Me through their word; that they all may be one, as You, Father, are in Me, and I in You; that they also may be one in Us, that the world may believe that You sent Me. And the glory which You gave Me I have given them, that they may be one just as We are one: I in them, and You in Me; that they may be made perfect in one, and that the world may know that You have sent Me, and have loved them as You have loved Me."

Have you ever wondered what this looks like? To be one not only with Jesus but also with the body of Christ?

Until recently, I did not fully comprehend the depth and richness of the word "unity" discussed in this passage, but each of you has made a tremendous impact on my journey here on earth. Through thoughts, prayers, and actions, you have defined "unity" and "being one" in the body of Christ. You have displayed the perfect unity around us that is in Jesus' prayer. Thank you and God bless you and your families, especially during this special time as we remember the reason for the season.

Specific prayer request if you have time:

- ➢ Complete healing and cleansing of all cancer cells by the power of the Holy Spirit.
- ➢ No complications.
- ➢ Family, faith, and hope to be uplifted.
- ➢ Full manifestation of God's gifts he has given to the healers He has placed on earth.
- ➢ For us to glorify God at all times.
- ➢ And for our family and friends to be in unity and be the light that shines for the Kingdom on earth during our stay at MD Anderson.

Thank you so much, we love each of you for the love, the care, and the patience you have given without expectation.

Have a very merry Jesus' birthday celebration!

Alan

December 20, 2010—Surgery Day

Inda, Tyler, Dustin, and I stayed at the Rotary House Hotel adjacent to MD Anderson and woke up bright and early, around 5:00 AM. My surgery was scheduled to last 8 to 9 hours. The night before, we had a nice dinner in the hotel. No one really knew what to say, which is unusual in our family. We laughed a lot and reminisced about silly things the boys did when they were young. Since I was still using my scooter to keep my left foot off the ground, my mobility was limited. I noticed a couple sitting in the dining room eating dinner. I supposed they were husband and wife. She had obviously gone through a significant amount of treatment. Her hair was gone. She was very thin. No laughter at the table. No apparent hope. They just sat there chewing their food, almost like they were waiting for death to come knocking on the door. I was sad for them and wondered if I might soon be sitting in their shoes, and in my heart of hearts, I did not want to!

> *Unless we are shaken and awakened, do we all have a tendency to let life consume us while we wait for death to come?*

A slow fade...unnoticeably gradual. We don't even know its taking place. Complacency. Discontentment. Unhappiness. Things used by the enemy to distract us from who God created us to be. Prior to cancer, I think this was who I had become. My life was going in a positive direction. I thought I had it pretty good. But even then I kept wondering, "Is this all there is to life?"

Waiting. Watching the ticking time clock until our time is done. The only difference between the majority of the population and myself is that the word cancer is staring smack-dab in my face. The word death is looming overhead and because of this unusual gift, I have a new perspective on life. I have become newly aware of how I can choose death...or life. No matter what happens, I have a choice. I can choose to be alive while I am here on this planet or I can walk around in death. It's my choice. And I believe that satan wants us to walk around in death, missing out on our divine purpose and the work God has called us to do.

"The Lord will fulfill his purpose for me; your steadfast love, O Lord, endures forever. Do not forsake the work of your hands." Psalm 138:8 ESV

I think joy and laughter push satan away and help give us life. Even in the midst of illness. Or unexpected circumstances. Or on a horrible, terrible, very bad day.

"A merry heart does good, like medicine, But a broken spirit dries the bones." Proverbs 17:22

As we walked (and I scooted) to the surgery prep area, we saw a huge Christmas tree in the lobby of MD Anderson. I bet that thing was 25 feet tall! We stopped to take pictures of the family in front of the tree, which to this day is one of my favorites. Although I could feel the temptation of fear and anxiety walking alongside me, I resisted and chose to walk with hope instead. I am blessed to have my family along for the ride!

HIDDEN BLESSINGS FROM CANCER

See my smile? That's a smile of trepidation.

December 20, 2010—A Post from Inda

We arrived at MD Anderson at 9:00 am this morning. After surgery prep, he went in at about 11:30 am. The surgery will take about 8 hours. He slept okay last night but woke up at 4:30 am. We have a room right across the street from the hospital.

His spirits are great; he really amazes me. So strong! We need lots of prayers today.

The boys are with me, as well as, a great college friend (the best man from our wedding). Alan's mom & sister will join us later this afternoon, along with a pastor from Promiseland West.

I just can't tell you how much your thoughts, prayers, posts, and acts of kindness have meant to us! It's like opening a Christmas gift every time we check this site! Thank you for showering us with your love and generosity!

ALAN WILLIAMS

December 21, 2010—A Post from Inda

Last night was remarkable! Alan was feeling great! The boys & I took turns taking shifts with Alan and after "sleeping" all day, he was wired for gab all night! Late night conversations can get really deep and spiritual when all is (relatively) quiet around you! We each enjoyed our own special time with him.

He's so strong! I just can't imagine how I'd feel after what he's been through! We are certain the worst is over and by the grace of God, we are expecting to learn that all of his removed lymph nodes are clear, as well as the tissue taken from his heel. It's just a matter of time before we'll have the proof! God is mighty and good!

Again, I can't thank you enough for your love, support, concern and especially your prayers! Alan has spent a good portion of the morning reading your posts and texts. The power of prayer is immeasurable and we are extremely blessed to have so many prayer warriors praying on our behalf!

Here are our prayer requests for today!

- Complete, miraculous healing of his leg and foot.
- No cancer to be found in any removed tissue.
- A complete cleansing of any cancer wandering around in his body.
- And finally, that we will be a warm and inviting light, reflecting the love of Christ to others here in the hospital as we celebrate the birth of our Christ!

Thank you, prayer warriors!!!!

Inda

December 22, 2010 — A Post from Inda

Yesterday was great. Alan's doing well both physically & spiritually. The boys hung with us through the late afternoon and left to join Alan's mom about an hour south of here. They spent the night with her helping out around the house. They're on their way here with her now. They will likely travel back to Austin today. It's so cool to watch them grow quickly in maturity as they try to anticipate our needs and fulfill them and yet, at the same time, clown around with blowing up surgical gloves like balloons! Always a source of joy & laughter!

Highlights from yesterday include sitting in a chair for a couple of hours and a very special visit from Jim Tolles and Robert Brewer, ending in a sweet prayer session with lots of brotherly love and camaraderie. Thank you, guys.

Today Alan was strong enough to get up & shower but it did take a toll & now he's just recovering.

We're watching his CK count - something in the blood that indicates damage done to muscle tissue. The chemotherapy treatment did a big number on the muscles in his leg. This number will peak and then subside before they will let him leave. This usually takes about 5 days. However, we have prayed over this process and fully expect its effects to be minimal!

So our prayer requests remain the same:

- ➢ *Complete, miraculous healing of his leg and foot.*
- ➢ *No cancer to be found in any removed tissue.*
- ➢ *A complete cleansing of any cancer wandering around in his body.*

> And finally, that we will be a warm and inviting light, reflecting the love of Christ to others here in the hospital as we celebrate the birth of our Lord and Savior!

Once again, thank you, prayer warriors!!!

Inda

December 23, 2010—A Post from Inda

Yesterday was awesome! Alan had a steady stream of visitors coming through to love on him and help him pass the time. It was rather exhausting but in a wonderful way! Brian even brought a decorated Norfolk pine to help us celebrate the season! Yesterday evening, we did get carried away and got behind on his pain meds. That caused a bit of a setback and a long, bummer of a night. Thankfully he's recovered nicely today and we're doing a better job of staying on top of it!

We did two laps around the nurse's station today and that was rather taxing. Alan's CK count in his blood is high (as expected), however, we don't know if its peaked. They put him back on his IV fluids to help with the swelling and to flush his blood some, along with a steroid. Dr. Ross said the earliest we will leave is Christmas day.

The boys went back to Austin yesterday afternoon for a break and to liberate the dogs from the kennel! Those guys have been going non-stop since Chance's wedding on the 18th. Laney reports that they were in the garden clearing it out for Alan! Wow! With all this cancer stuff, we're really looking forward to our own organic veggies!

So at the end of the day, Alan is a happy camper, praising God, and enjoying the awesome love and support showered on him by our family, friends, and the staff here at MD. God is so good!

- ➢ Prayer requests: CK count has peaked and no complications.

December 24, 2010—A Post from Inda

Wow, Alan's a happy camper today! He woke up feeling great and was alert & active all day! His CK count is still high, but not unusual; the last draw only went up about 3%. Maybe a plateau? Physical therapy came by and worked him over! Dr. Ross says Alan's healing is amazing!

His family surprised him with a visit and the boys made it in this evening despite the storm and an iffy battery! He's so happy to be spending the night before Christmas with his boys. (Me, too!) There's a good chance we'll get to go home tomorrow.

I have to do a shout out for MD. This place is awesome! Especially at Christmas! There is a Christmas tree around every corner, nurses, and volunteers wearing Christmas hats, and even an ensemble of thirteen trombones, a tuba, and cello was playing Christmas carols today. The Christmas spirit just floods the halls and rooms and fills everyone with such joy! It's just great!

Reflection:

Months after my surgeries, Mike Murphy, the man of God mentioned earlier in this story, told me that it was Inda's faith that healed me. I did not understand what he meant. How could Inda's faith heal me? The gift of faith is referenced in 1 Corinthians 12:9 as a spiritual gift, albeit it is not very well explained. Again, I may not be able to fully or adequately expound, but I felt Inda's continued presence and extraordinary confidence in the promises and power of God. She repeatedly affirmed that she would stay beside me, and she believed God had and would continue to heal me. Her faith was unshakable and strong, which edified me when I was emotionally unraveling. She used positive, uplifting words, even when I struggled and didn't say anything positive in return. She never personified cancer as being mine. She was my Noah who built an ark when nobody had ever heard of rain. She was my Abraham who believed he would have a son when it was impossible. She was heaven sent!!!! Please see her book when it is released in summer 2016, **The Power of a Caregiver** for more information about her journey.

December 25, 2010—During the Drive Home from Houston to Austin

Merry Christmas to each of you and your families as we all celebrate Jesus' birthday! It has been a very Merry Christmas for us as well! Dr. Ross released me today to return home to Austin. I was extremely ready to leave the hospital, but at the same time, I treasured the extensive care I was receiving from Dr. Ross, his team, and the people at MD Anderson. Inda has been updating this site since the surgery, mainly because the invasiveness of the surgery and the toll it took on me physically. Words cannot describe how incredibly awesome she is! And I cannot portray how blessed I feel with two sons who rallied around Inda and me like they have the last few weeks. They displayed an unexplainable joy and uplifting spirit that only Christ in them could manifest. One of the most amusing things they did was to sneak into my room Christmas Eve, pretending to be Santa for me. I caught them in the act, but it was so funny seeing them set the presents around the miniature Christmas tree that Brian brought. My mom, sister, and her family have also been incredibly supportive in comfort and accommodations. Thank you so much! Friends have called, texted, posted, visited, emailed, and communicated support, prayers, and encouragement throughout this process and each one has made a significant impact on our lives. You have pumped up our faith and positive assurances. Thank you so much for uplifting and enriching our lives. **I absolutely know that your prayers have made an impact on how things have progressed.**

"Is anyone among you sick? Let him call for the elders of the church, and let them pray over him, anointing him with oil in the name of the Lord. **And the prayer of faith will save the one who is sick**, and the Lord will raise him up. And if he has committed sins, he will be forgiven." James 5:14-15 *(Emphasis mine)*

Physical update:

Dr. Ross and team attacked the potential cancer cells in my leg and they did it very thoroughly and aggressively, which I very much appreciated! The third day after surgery, he said he was amazed at how well the healing was progressing...thanks to prayer! However, my leg has swollen considerably and my knee is extremely limited in the range of motion to about 20% of normal. They cut and split an upper inner thigh muscle so that I would have coverage over the arteries in my leg where the lymph nodes were removed. They removed more of my heel; hence, I will not be able to walk on it for a few more weeks. I have drain tubes hanging out of my leg, leading to a container that I will have with me for some time. In short, I have limited mobility and, according to Dr. Ross, I should regain use of my leg in different stages over the next 8-12 weeks. To complain would be an insult to the other patients and their struggles, as well as, to the integrity of the unbelievably complicated work occurring at MD Anderson! I have been deeply impacted by the impact of cancer on the lives of others and yet, deeply moved by their positive attitudes. The patients are truly grateful for each breath they take.

Over the next few months, my primary treatment is to wait for healing to take place. My stitches and tubes will be removed in approximately three weeks, and I may be allowed to put some pressure on my foot. Also, I hopefully will have a significant reduction in inflammation, which would increase flexibility. Simultaneously, we will be seeking God's guidance in determining what treatment, if any, we will do in the future. Possible treatments are interferon or an experimental vaccine if I qualify.

Spiritual Update:

Seems like whenever I try to bless someone, instead, I am the one humbled and blessed. In my last post, I mentioned that I wanted our family to bring the spirit of Christmas to MD Anderson. I tried to be a good patient and be a positive influence and I think we did an adequate job, but to my surprise, the people at MD already had it going on! God placed the healers where they needed to be, the encouragers in their right places, the ones with gifts of service in their respective spots, and the ones expressing comfort readily available. God's presence was already there. Brightly shining. Wherever I turned. Although I presumed that it was my job, God was already there and working mightily! People. Doctors. Nurses.

Workers. Servers. Wherever I looked, I could see Jesus working there. The joy of the Lord was evident amongst the staff working Christmas Eve and Christmas day. Volunteers showed up Christmas morning with presents for the patients. I received a gift card and a stuffed bear that I will treasure for years. The people were extraordinarily uplifting. Volunteers hosted a free turkey and dressing lunch with all the fixings for patients and their families with live Christmas music. It was awesome, uniting all of us facing similar circumstances! I was humbled to look around the cafeteria at the various IV trees (trees of life as the boys called them) and the support groups surrounding each one.

Jessica, the lady who helped with my physical therapy, said my chart was noted as an "urgent, must modify behavior" because I was told to ask for help if I needed to get out of bed, but was caught trying to hop around on one foot and jump on my scooter. She was also helping a lady who was not expected to live for more than a few more hours. It was obvious she loved her job. She loved well. She encouraged others. I was inspired by how much she cared.

Over and over and over again, I felt the support of people and prayer during my time of surgery and recovery! According to Dr. Ross, my recovery has been very quick with considerably less impact compared with others he has seen. He even used the word "amazing." I have always been one to do things for myself, to take the ball and run with it, and be the man. However, during this last week, I learned something new...I learned to accept the help and prayer support of others. You willingly and joyfully gave it and I welcomed it. It worked! We felt it! Prior to this experience, I think I was too proud to ask for or accept the help of others. I didn't want to make myself seem vulnerable as a man in this world. I doubted how much we, the body of Christ, could accomplish when we lived in unity with one other as God intended. I didn't understand the breadth, the depth, the width, and the height of God's love that becomes apparent when we share and help each other. I now understand why John 17 so deeply impacted me earlier this year. Jesus prayed for us to live in unity so that the kingdom will be revealed. God is awesome and so are His people, especially when we unite with each other! And this is my prayer for you as well.

> "The goal is for all of them to become one heart and mind—
> Just as you, Father, are in me and I in you,
> So they might be one heart and mind with us.
> Then the world might believe that you, in fact, sent me.
> The same glory you gave me, I gave them,
> So they'll be as unified and together as we are—
> I in them and you in me.
> Then they'll be mature in this oneness,
> And give the godless world evidence
>
> That you've sent me and loved them
> In the same way you've loved me." John 17:21-23 MSG

Please pray for the healers, servers, encouragers, and bearers of the Spirit of God to continue their work at MD Anderson and the other health facilities in which they work. Pray for each other continually. Personally, please pray for continued and complete healing and cleansing with no complications. Also, please pray for me to have discernment regarding my future treatment decisions.

Thank you again and I love you all!

Alan

December 28, 2010

Praise God and thank you prayer warriors! I received a phone call from the lab at MD Anderson today and all lymph nodes and heel margin came back negative for melanoma. Thanks to you and the Holy Spirit, the tests came back exactly how we prayed for.

You are awesome! So is God!! Alan

Celebration dinner! Tyler's birthday and my test results!

ALAN WILLIAMS

9 | RESTING IN SPIRITUAL AWARENESS

Inda and I entered into a season of rest and recovery following my second surgery. I strongly feel that when our minds are preoccupied with the things to come, we miss out on the moments that God has for us now. A spiritual mentor, George Oaks, once said to me, "satan wants our mind to be in the future or the past, not the present." During the three months from my first diagnosis through my second surgery, a spiritual awareness occurred and I realized the closeness of the spiritual realm. It is much closer than I ever imagined! If we let our minds drift too far into the future, we miss the immanence of the Holy Spirit working in our midst today. When our thoughts are consumed by worry, anxiety, and our own well-being, we unknowingly attach strings. We place expectations on God, telling Him how to do certain things. I expect to grow old with the love of my life. I expect to hold grandchildren in my lap and push them on the swing. I expect to have health and prosperity (at least, to some extent). When I have the courage to be honest, these are the things I think I deserve.

God is so good! I can enjoy spending time with my granddaughter.

Expectations creep in and kill relationships, with God and our fellow man.

When I don't get what I expect I deserve, I befriend anger, jealousy, and resentment. Love and joy are pushed out, leaving me feeling mad and upset. I no longer can enjoy the moment I am living in.

When our lives are emptied, we become surprised how full we truly are.

What are my expectations? The things that once mattered to me became trivial. Survival and relationships went like a rocket ship to the top of my priority list. My purpose in life made a monumental shift. Each day, each breath was a brand new gift.

The sky.

The clouds.

A butterfly.

A cardinal.

The insignificantly small details I had long overlooked suddenly spoke volumes to me. I saw everything as an undeserved gift. As I gazed at my surroundings, I was overwhelmed by the gift of grace. I was able to see God's gift of life abounding.

The Apostle Paul really began to challenge me. Here is a guy who was beaten, falsely accused, and imprisoned, and yet, he wrote love letters from God to us. I found this quite perplexing! Putting myself in his shoes, I imagined sitting in sewage, aching from head to toe from physical ailments, and longing to be set free. However, despite his mistreatment, he doesn't complain about his circumstances but instead, says to count it all joy. Count it all joy. It appears as a far-fetched dichotomy. Paul is my hero because the things he went through were much worse than mine and he didn't let his physical circumstances stop him. Some of the people I saw at MD Anderson were in horrific condition. Some gave in to their circumstances and looked like they had given up while others were incredibly joyful and full of life. The joy of some was astonishing. I asked myself, "Could I live grateful to God for every small gift? Could I live grateful with the seemingly impossible?"

And some of those I encountered were terribly disfigured due to the surgeries and treatment they went through. I wondered if they had looked in a mirror lately. I wondered how in the world did they find such joy? Faces half removed. Some kind of skin replacement. Body parts gone missing. Baffling as it sounds, some of them were fully alive and thriving within, while others looked almost dead. I wondered why the wide range of disparity in these people. Some had an unfathomable presence of hope. Some looked like they were just waiting to die. To simply live out the diagnosis given to them without a fight.

Seven years earlier, our family went on a mission trip to Mexico to build a plywood house for a family. The foundation was built on cinder blocks and had six 4' x 8' sheets of plywood as a floor. Compared to the surrounding homes that housed up to eight family members, this was a mansion. At the end of the construction week, we gave the children in our newly built home a soccer ball. We had noticed they didn't have any toys. Within minutes, all the children in the small village came out to play with the soccer ball. Apparently soccer balls and toys are a hot commodity. I could not wrap my mind around all the joy and laughter over one puny soccer ball as they kicked it around to each other. At first, I thought how ridiculous that was. Why didn't their parents buy them something as small as a soccer ball? I began to see the joy and laughter explode in a relatively lifeless community. While working for the past few days, I had not heard a sound from these children. No laughter. No playing. Nothing at all.

It's such a joy to bring some joy!

I recalled from one of our training classes that suicide rates in the U.S. were much higher than in this small village in Mexico with no running water. They lived within muddy, trash composed walls covered by a tin roof, which provided a home for an entire family sleeping in an 8' x 8' space with dirt floors. Maybe 4 feet in height. Outhouses that flooded and overflowed constantly.

And I wondered how I would do in this place.

And I wondered why the difference in suicide rates. Was it due to unrealistic or unmet expectations that we impose on ourselves in the U.S.? Was it because these people were more focused on survival rather than some non-life essential comfort? Was it because this village found happiness in each other?

I pondered this thought for the next couple of days. I began to relate my circumstances to their situation. I began making a choice to live. My circumstances would no longer define me. My chance of survival was not a death sentence, but instead, an opportunity to persevere through to the end. Then I see it come to life in this passage of Scripture:

"Not only so, but we also glory in our sufferings, because we know that suffering produces perseverance; perseverance, character; and character, hope. And hope does not put us to shame, because God's love has been poured out into our hearts through the Holy Spirit, who has been given to us. You see, at just the right time, when we were still powerless, Christ died for the ungodly." Romans 5:3-6 NIV

Sure, I had read this passage before. But this time, it took on new life. The words that were written here leaped off the page...it is the suffering that produces hope! I dig for my dictionary desiring to learn and what I discover is a long lost treasure. The word for hope is *elpis*, meaning to expect or anticipate, usually with pleasure. I could hear the Holy Spirit speaking to me. It's because of Jesus I have a new life; without Him I am a lost sinner. Because of my suffering, I have a newfound expectation...**God is up to something!**

God's Word tells us to "Love the Lord your God with all your heart, with all your soul, with all your strength, and with all your mind" (Luke 10:27). I knew I was supposed to fall in love with God. I get that. He is right there beside me. I've been told about God's omnipresence many times before. Consequently, I never really thought about how close the enemy is to me as well. He is closer than I ever imagined or dreamed. *But*, satan can be defeated. As a believer, we have the upper hand. satan may be sneaking around like a roaring lion, seeking whom he may devour (1 Peter 5:8), but we can be aware.

> *"...in order that Satan might not outwit us. For we are not unaware of his schemes." 2 Corinthians 2:11 NIV*

satan attempts to outsmart us, but we can beat him at his game. The word "outwit" is from the Greek word *pleonekteo*[7], meaning "to gain or take advantage of another, to overreach" through some

---

[7] "Pleonekteo" Def. 2. *Bible Tools Online*. Strong's #4122: Pleonekteo - Greek/Hebrew Definitions - Bible Tools. November 13, 2012. Accessed June 07, 2016.
http://www.bibletools.org/index.cfm/fuseaction/Lexicon.show/ID/G4122/pleonekteo.htm.

sinister or sneaky means. It is a compound word of *pleion*[8], meaning "more," and *echo*[9], meaning "to be addicted to." So, in other words, it denotes an insatiable appetite of the enemy to have more, more, and more. Make no mistake, he is a greedy guy. He is our enemy who wants nothing more than to defeat us, destroy us, overtake us, and ultimately take us captive. Knowing this is a game changer! We don't have to let him win!

---

[8] "Pleion" Def. 1a). *Bible Tools Online*. Strong's #4119: Pleion - Greek/Hebrew Definitions - Bible Tools. November 13, 2012. Accessed June 07, 2016. http://www.bibletools.org/index.cfm/fuseaction/Lexicon.show/ID/G4119/pleion.htm.

[9] "Prosecho" Def. 4a. *Bible Tools Online*. Strongs's #4337: Prosecho - Greek/Hebrew Definitions - Bible Tools. November 13, 2012. Accessed June 07, 2016. http://www.bibletools.org/index.cfm/fuseaction/Lexicon.show/ID/G4337/prosecho.htm.

ALAN WILLIAMS

10 | FINDING PEACE

I knew I had a long journey ahead of recovery and treatment, but day-by-day, I was learning how to find "the peace that surpasses all understanding" in the midst of my suffering. God's peace and comfort are something only He can provide. It is extraordinary. In the same manner, whatever difficulty you are currently facing doesn't have to defeat you. satan will mess with your relationships, business, family, finances, plans—anything—to find ways to destroy or distract you from what you hold dear. Instead of fretting over your situation, God asks you to trust Him with your everything. He sent us the Holy Spirit as our Comforter and Helper to open our eyes. The enemy is working all around us. We don't want to let him pull the wool over our eyes. He is a crafty creature (Genesis 3:1), but we do not need to fall prey to his wicked schemes. When in these dire circumstances, we should hold on tight to God's promise of peace!

"You will keep him in perfect peace, Whose mind is stayed on You, Because he trusts in You." Isaiah 26:3

The next season was a struggle at times, but I would not trade it for anything! I brought many struggles on myself and hope others may gain perspective in order to avoid my same pitfalls. But no matter what I brought on myself, God pulled me through. He loves me and He loves you. He loves us all as we love Him and receive His love! Wherever we are. Regardless of our current situation and circumstances. He is able to turn anything around. He is able to put our feet on solid ground.

> *"He lifted me out of the slimy pit, out of the mud and mire; he set my feet on a rock and gave me a firm place to stand."*
> *Psalm 40:2 NIV*

If you recall the story of Joseph, it is a twisted tale with many ups and downs. He is beloved by his father Jacob and due to such favoritism, wickedly hated by his older brothers. Their jealousy grew to the point where they wanted him dead. One day while they were out tending their sheep, Joseph comes towards them. With intense hatred brewing in their hearts, they scheme about ways to kill their brother but in the end, sell him into slavery. Joseph winds up in Egypt working for the Pharaoh. To make a long story short, we see his journey riddled with injustice, ultimately landing him in jail. Years later he is released because he interprets a dream. He rises again in power, directing the nation of Egypt and the Pharaoh through a famine. Ultimately, he is reunited with his brothers. We watch his story unfold. Upon seeing their faces, one would assume he would be riddled with bitterness and anger for all that was done to him. But, oh no. We see a sovereign God who was intricately weaving the pieces, telling a greater story than we could unfold.

Upon seeing the faces of his brothers, Joseph says, *"As for you, you meant evil against me, but God meant it for good, to bring it about that many people should be kept alive, as they are today." Genesis 50:20 ESV*

God tells the greatest stories. What satan intends for evil, God is working together for our good. As long as we are walking with Jesus, our destination is not what satan would have us think. Though my experience with cancer hasn't been easy, it certainly has been for my good. My faith has grown. Relationships have deepened. My understanding of God's Word has reached a greater depth. I have participated in God's work for the benefit of others. This life on earth is an incredible adventure that, I believe, satan deceived me into thinking would be no fun as a Christian. But let me tell you something, my adventure with Jesus has been more exciting than I could've ever imagined! And to the glory of God, my journey on earth has just begun.

ALAN WILLIAMS

11 | PAUSING TO REFLECT

Once cancer is diagnosed, or for that matter, any tragedy in life is exposed--whether it affects health, finances, or relationships--whatever--I know that finding peace and rest is difficult. I, too, have been through them all. Finding God's personal answer (not the instructions of family, friends, doctors, or self-help gurus) is the key to our physical and emotional healing, wholeness, and restoration. He is with us and for us. Doctors kept telling me about various scenarios concerning what was coming up ahead. The next. Then next. Then what if? Thoughts of confusion and fear were crowding my head. Thankfully, a good friend reminded me to think about the **next best step**, rather than the "What ifs?" or possible disastrous outcomes. My thoughts continued to wander, wanting to focus on the bad. It was a constant fight to reel them in.

But if I have one piece of advice to give you: Rest in the season you are in.

God has lessons hidden in trials if we trust Him. And I found peace of mind when I prayed and began listening and hearing answers in this adventure. In this season, I hung onto a certain Bible verse found in Romans. The more I go into deeper dependence on God, the greater depth I discover in this verse, which is why I have fallen in love with this transformational adventure.

"And we know that all things work together for good to those who love God, to those who are the called according to His purpose." Romans 8:28

HIDDEN BLESSINGS FROM CANCER

ALAN WILLIAMS

ABOUT THE AUTHOR

Alan Williams was raised in Lake Jackson, Texas. He attended the University of Texas in Austin, lettered three years as a UT Longhorn offensive lineman, and graduated with a Bachelor's degree in Finance. There he also met the love of his life, Inda. Alan began a banking career, rising to become one of Austin's youngest VPs in lending. He left banking and later became the youngest partner in an insurance firm of seventy partners. After 15 years in commercial insurance, God called him to embark on a career Alan said he'd never do – become an operator of a restaurant. He now operates two restaurants.

Alan has served and ministered to the community through the Lake Travis Zoning and Planning District, the Lake Travis Parks and Recreation Board and the Lake Travis ISD School Board. He daily mentors his employees and serves the City of Austin as an ambassador to Christ Together Greater Austin. He has served in various church committees including Finance Team Chair at Life Austin Church. His personal mission is to "Be a spark that ignites and unites our nation under God."

Alan and his wife, Inda, of thirty-four years reside in Austin, Texas and have two incredible sons, their beautiful wives, and a granddaughter who lights up their world!

ALAN WILLIAMS

ABOUT THE CONTRIBUTING WRITER

Sue A. Allen resides in Austin, Texas along with her husband and four overly active children ranging in age from four to nineteen (the youngest who was adopted from Haiti). She loves encouraging people to "Go live your story for God's glory—you will certainly enjoy the ride!" For the past 15 years, Sue has enjoyed serving her local church in various capacities, including teaching in women's ministry, leading adult bible study, and guiding short-term mission trips. Her newly released women's Bible study, "I Didn't Want to be That Girl! A Look into the Life of Eve" is now available.

Sue, along with her husband Coby, founded Dell Children's Medical Global Outreach, which provides much needed medical care and training to underserved populations around the world. She also serves on the board of MyLifeSpeaks, a missions organization located in rural Haiti which is focused on serving the "least of these." To find out more, please visit Sue's blog at www.sueaallen.com.

ALAN WILLIAMS

MORE STORIES

Transformational Adventures is a series of stories about the lessons of hope and victory learned through the life journey of Alan & Inda Williams. God has placed it on their hearts to share these stories to bring hope and empowerment to those that are going through life's devastating challenges such as disease, mishaps or just a state of dis-ease.

Stories published are:

The Heart Of It All

Stories to come are:

Hidden Blessings from Chemo
The Power of a Caregiver
Transformed Relationships
Cancer Again
Serving at Work and Community

Please join us on our website as we continually add videos and additional information regarding this adventure at:

TransformationalAdventure.com

ALAN WILLIAMS

The Heart of It All
Available Now on Amazon

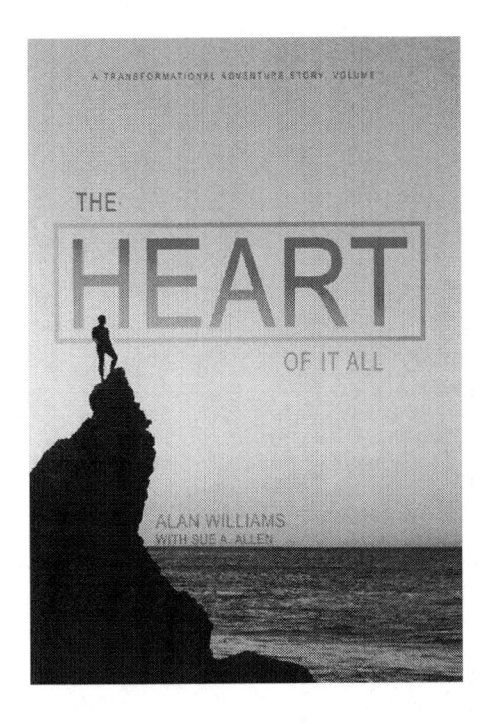

"I was used to being the leader: The guy with the football scholarship, the rising young professional, the head of a beautiful family. I had it all...or so I thought.

After months of chest pain, I found myself lying on a table in a doctor's office. I heard my nurse cuss underneath his breath. He was staring at an angiogram of my heart and it looked deadly.

Between the stress tests and the angiogram, my cardiologist revealed that I had two 90 degree bends in my Left Anterior Descending Artery. It was 98% blocked, and most other patients in my condition wouldn't be alive.

Within five years, I had two heart surgeries.... one physical and one spiritual.

I am a miracle. What He's done has blown me away....and it's available for all of us."

- Alan Williams
TransformationalAdventure.com

ALAN WILLIAMS

Hidden Blessings From Chemo
Coming Summer 2016

"Some say that faith requires you to 'get out of the boat' - but for me, faith looked like getting out of bed and getting *into* a boat.

When the doctor told me that I would be in bed for a year, my wife and I decided to develop a bucket list. These goals gave me hope.

I started sculling - and with the dosage of chemotherapy that I was receiving - I shouldn't have been able to do it...But I did.

I want to share with you how I made it through the worst part of chemo treatments and how I went from being fearful to thankful in daily living."

- Alan Williams
TransformationalAdventure.com

The Power of a Caregiver
Coming Fall 2016

"INDA, I HAVE CANCER."

My best friend and husband had dropped a bombshell on me.
I found myself stunned...but not powerless.
God had prepared me for this challenge.

FINDING HOPE

"When I heard Alan say "I have cancer," a wave of fear rolled over me. It sent my insides spinning.

After the initial shock of hearing about Alan's cancer, I knew everything was about to change. We had lived self-sufficient lives. We could do it all on our own. But this was bigger than we were - We couldn't work our way out of this one. We knew we were going to need some help.

Even though it was difficult, I found strength, learned how to master the waves of change, and provided support and care to my husband...It changed everything for our family, our marriage, and even Alan's health. I want to share with you what influenced and anchored me during one of the most challenging times of our lives."

- *Inda Williams*
TransformationalAdventure.com

ALAN WILLIAMS

HIDDEN BLESSINGS FROM CANCER

Made in the USA
San Bernardino, CA
07 May 2017